SUSAN BREEKS OF HELBECK

Victorian Ladies in Australia, India and Westmorland

Susan Breeks at Helbeck in old age

SUSAN BREEKS OF HELBECK

Victorian Ladies in Australia, India and Westmorland

Rosemary Blackett-Ord

HAYLOFT PUBLISHING LTD

First published by Hayloft Publishing Ltd., 2015

Hayloft Publishing Ltd, South Stainmore,
Kirkby Stephen, Cumbria, CA17 4DJ

tel: 017683 41568 or 07971 352473
email: books@hayloft.eu
web: www.hayloft.eu

ISBN 978 1 910237 05 2

A Catalogue record for this book is available from The British Library

Designed, printed and bound in the EU

Papers used by Hayloft are natural, recyclable products made from wood grown
in sustainable forests. The manufacturing processes conform to the environmental
regulations of the country of origin.

Jacket painting, 'Helbeck Hall' by David Cox, June 1867

This book is dedicated to Helbeck

List of Plates

Contents

Acknowledgments

I was as usual at Helbeck when I was starting to think of the many people who deserved thanks for their help with this book. I was listening to the choir of St David's Cathedral. It brought to mind at once the librarian and musician Tim Penton. He was introduced to me as a university friend of my eldest son Charles over forty years ago. He was the first to give me active help in arranging this story,

Before that time I had assembled most of my information for the book. Bill Hornby and the Mason-Hornby family had lent me the letters and journals which describe the descent of Susan Breeks from the Hornby family and the Stanleys of Knowsley and Elizabeth Farren the actress.

Daisy Thompson, who features in the text, and who was brought up by Jim Breeks's sisters, I met as an old lady. She was a close friend of my mother-in-law Lena Blackett-Ord, who died in 1961, and from each of them I learnt about Susan's life and family.

Much more recently Enid Laidlaw endlessly retyped the final versions of the text for me, and Joanne MacAlister and Angela Dargue kept the dust off my many heaps of paper. Support was given me by my late husband Jim Blackett-Ord, and by my sons Charles, Mark and Ben and my daughter Nicky Rawlence. Other help was given me by Christine Akrigg, Christina Bainbridge, John and Sarah Blackett-Ord, Lady Bourne, Hugo Bovill, Betsy Festing, Tony Ford, Andy Goldsworthy, Bishop A. K. K. Graham, Leni Griffiths, Judith Heelis, Lady Henderson, Sir Launcelot Henderson, Anthony Hobson, Lady Holdgate (Elizabeth), Bill Hornby, Mr H.O.R. Hornby, Lady Inglewood, Anne Lewis, Belinda Lyon-Smith, George McAllister, Joanne McAllister, Anne Smyth-Osborne, Major Harry Porter, Sheila Scott, Sir Reginald Seconde, Lady Rose Stephenson, Sandra Strong, Ian Tod, Joy Thompson, Raleigh Trevelyan and Caroline Dawnay.

I owe particular gratitude to my publisher Dawn Robertson and to many others too numerous to list who have helped me with a work that I began sixty years ago. I hope that I will be forgiven if I have failed to mention them all by name.

Ro Blackett-Ord
Helbeck,
May 2014.

Foreword

My mother Ro Blackett-Ord died on 23 May 2014, soon after the final manuscript of this book had been delivered to the publisher.

She was born in 1923, the daughter of E W Bovill, the distinguished historian of English country life, of the East India Company and of the Sahara Desert. In the War she joined the Wrens. When she was twenty she fell in love and quickly become engaged to my father Jim Blackett-Ord. He departed almost immediately to the battle of Anzio and a German prisoner of war camp. He returned in May 1945 in a poor state of nerves which she cured by marrying him within exactly a month.

She had known from before her marriage that the Helbeck estate was to come to him as the heir to his cousins the Breeks's. When she first set foot in Helbeck Hall she thought it cold, damp, dilapidated, lonely and haunted. But on her second visit, in 1951, when it had been emptied of furniture, and she had seen the garden, she was entranced. Still in her twenties she adopted wholesale my father's ambition to preserve it and live there.

Turning over the relics that had been left behind by the Breeks family, she had found one of them to be a book of carbon-copies of the letters of Susan Breeks who had lived at Helbeck in the 1890s. They became the foundation of this book.

After my father's death in 2012 she herself lived alone at Helbeck as a widow. But by Easter this year her mind was obviously failing. A crisis put her into the Carleton Unit at Carlisle. There she was soon a favourite with the inmates and nurses. She remained good-humoured and optimistic, intrigued by matters of interest to her, even if the matters were in fact wholly imaginary.

She died quietly in her sleep nearly a month after her ninety-first birthday.

Mark Blackett-Ord
October 2014

1

Helbeck

One day during the autumn of 1953, a large van arrived at Helbeck Hall, Westmorland. It contained one hundred and fifty heads and horns of game, three marble busts, a number of daguerreotypes, an elephant's ear, several elephant feet and half a dozen ancient Indian spears. When all this had been unloaded we also found two tin boxes containing account books, letters from India written during the last century, a map of the Nilgiris Hills and a miscellaneous collection of papers.

In the bottom of one of the tin boxes were two well-worn leather books. These contained fine leaves of tissue paper, being the carbon copies of letters, some written from India, others from Helbeck. The letters from India were written by Jim Breeks between 1868 and 1871, and those from Helbeck by his widow, Susan Breeks, between 1895 and 1901. The letters were difficult to read, the carbon being so pale and the paper transparent, but they were interesting in that they described the everyday life of the times. However, only some of the letters made sense as names and places meant nothing to me.

It must have been a year or two later when we were driving down the Great North Road that my husband and I saw a signpost to Ossington. I remembered the name from Susan Breeks's letters, so we followed the road and found Ossington Hall. The house was 18th century, large and imposing, and built of red brick. By asking in the village, we discovered that a Colonel Denison lived there. Susan Breeks had been a Denison before she married Jim Breeks.

Very shortly after this, I chanced to walk into Sotheby's sale rooms and saw that a large collection of books belonging to Colonel Denison of Ossington Hall were to be sold. The books were all on fishing. That afternoon I wrote to Colonel Denison. His reply was so encouraging that this, together with some good luck and research, has enabled me to discover who was who in the Denison family.

My husband, Jim Blackett-Ord, had unexpectedly inherited Helbeck Hall in 1951. We had seen the house some years previously on a wet and cold winter's day. Inside, chickens were running about on the ground floor, wallpaper was hanging off the walls and the downstairs was painted dark brown and 'battleship' grey. It was deeply gloomy, but I consoled myself with the thought that Jim would not inherit for many years. In fact, Aunt Olive Breeks died in 1951, two weeks after her daughter Audrey. They were probably killed by the noxious fumes which came through the grating at the bottom of the stairs from the coke furnace which was the sole form of heating. In fact, no warmth came from the furnace below. The estate was then due to pass to another widow, but she said she "didn't want to live in that old place."

Jim and I came up from London on a bright, sunny day and were captivated by the 'Strawberry Hill' ogee windows. The paper was still hanging off the walls in the rooms and rain had come in nearly everywhere. There was no furniture, no rugs and no curtains, though a few dark blue blinds of an earlier age hung over some of the windows. An old Calor gas cooker stood near the large, old range in the kitchen and bells for all the rooms hung along the top of one of the kitchen walls. The house was very cold indeed.

Needless to say, the farmhouses and cottages on the estate were in need of repair, fences were broken and gates were painted on one side only. Derelict is the only way to describe everything.

Later, I had a chance meeting with an Anthony Mason-Hornby whilst shooting grouse. As a result of this meeting, he lent me the contents of a small tin box he owned, which contained the most exciting letters, notes and papers of the well-known 18th century actress, Elisabeth Farren, who became the second wife of the 12th Earl of Derby, and also letters of the Hornby families, written during the first quarter of the 19th century. All these people were ancestors of Lady Denison, Susan Breeks's mother. They were as exciting as the postcard I later received from Tony Mason-Hornby which said "publish and photograph anything you like."

I appeared to be delving back from Breeks to Denison and further back to Hornby, for Susan's mother, Lina Denison was a Hornby; and finally to General Burgoyne, whose illegitimate daughter Maria married Phipps Hornby. Susan Breeks of Helbeck was the great granddaughter of General Burgoyne, so it is with him that this story starts.

The characters in the story were typical of their time. They are not exciting or important, or even nasty, but they give us glimpses into their thoughts and ideals and how they lived. All of them, from General John Burgoyne, who lived in the 18th century, to Susan Breeks in the 19th century, wrote innumerable letters, almost always written within the family circle to each other. They also kept diaries and notebooks, thus giving us a fascinating insight into the way that life changed and they changed with it.

The Right Honourable General John Burgoyne, Eliza Farren, the well-known actress, and the 12th Earl of Derby were uncomplicated, sometimes brash, but entirely genuine people who might have come out of a Mozart opera or a Fragonard picture. There is a touch of lightness in their lives and an immensely attractive attitude to life, which in many ways, was highly immoral. It was then in no way strange that, following the death of General Burgoyne, his three illegitimate children were taken from their mother, Susan Caulfield, a singer, and were brought up by Lord Derby at Knowsley, the home of the General's deceased wife, Charlotte. His daughter, Maria Sophia, was the grandmother of Susan Breeks.

2

General John Burgoyne

John Burgoyne, later General Burgoyne, and James Stanley, the heir to Lord Derby, were often seen together in the coffee houses and at the gambling tables of the elite in London. In 1740 they had both left Westminster School. They shared a passion for cockfighting, which also went on at Knowsley, the palatial house in Lancashire which was the Derby family home.

The good looking, flamboyant John had a passion for the theatre and, curiously, for the army, and was always extravagantly dressed. When they were at Knowsley, John fell in love with James Stanley's youngest sister, Lady Charlotte Stanley.

Lord Derby would not hear of his daughter marrying an impoverished soldier, so the young couple eloped to London where they were married at St George's Chapel in Curzon Street on 14th April 1743. In spite of his disapproval, Lord Derby gave Charlotte a small dowry with which Burgoyne was able to buy a Captaincy in the 13th Dragoons.

For the well-to-do, London was a fascinating place in which to live. However, St James's Street and all the other main thoroughfares through London were filthy and noisy because of the carts, carriages and every other mode of conveyance which rattled over the cobblestones. Only the sedan chair was a quiet way to travel the then small area of St James's which made up the centre of London.

Added to the dust, dirt and the noise were the constant cries of the costermongers and the gin drinkers who habituated the numerous alleys. It was almost as noisy as it is today. Mob violence would erupt at the slightest provocation. There were no police, and only on rare occasions were the militia called in. Bow Street runners were not yet known, and when the howls of the mob came near to any of the large houses, the only thing to do was to hand out free ale and shut all the shutters. At St James's Palace, the King complained of the dust and dirt and was considering buying Buckingham House, which was in the country near Hyde Park. Lord Stanley's house was on the new, fashionable edge of town in Grosvenor Square. Beyond Park Lane was the countryside.

All this in no way prevented the rich from enjoying themselves, and enjoy themselves they did. Men wore beautifully embroidered and brightly coloured clothes which matched or contrasted with the colours of the ladies' silk dresses; for at that time, beautiful golds, silvers and lace were in fashion.

However, when the Burgoynes were in London, there were debts to be paid, so after three years they went to live in the village of Chantiloup in France where they could live more cheaply. We can infer, from a surviving letter written by the General

in later life to Charlotte's niece, Lady Elisabeth ('Betty') Stanley, that they were a
very happy couple:

> She was, in the younger part of her life, as industrious as she was excellent in
> every useful and elegant employment. She much loved work as an amusement
> and we lived during those best years in a country where attentions were not solely
> attached to expense and outward appearance, but where one maid, one man and
> a cook of three pounds a year made all our household; but whenever we pleased
> we could sally from our Hash and Potatoes, to brilliant circles and refined luxury
> and the politest conversation of Europe.

They stayed in France for four years and then moved to Rome. It was in Rome that
Alan Ramsey painted Burgoyne's portrait. In 1755 they were in Florence where they
mixed with the other English people. Robert Adam used to dance with Charlotte. "She
didn't like the foreigners; she dances charmingly," he said.

At the outbreak of the Seven Years War in 1756, the Burgoynes returned to England
where John raised the 1st Light Cavalry Regiment and by 1761, he was in Parliament
as MP for Midhurst in Kent. The following year, as a Brigadier General, when Spain
invaded Portugal, he distinguished himself commanding the British troops during the
relief of Portugal.

Burgoyne returned home to find that his old friend James Stanley had died while he
had been away. The General and Charlotte befriended, and appear to have more or less
adopted, James's children. They had no children of their own, and the Burgoynes spent
part of their time at Knowsley, Charlotte's old home.

Edward Stanley, Charlotte's nephew, in particular, admired his uncle the General.
Perhaps there was a hint of hero worship by the young Edward for his lovable, perhaps
one could say adventurous, uncle who was such a close friend of his father. During
the following years, General Burgoyne, as he now was, and his nephew were seen together in society, just as the General and Edward's father had been seen together many
years earlier. An incongruous pair, for one was thirty years older than the other.

In later years, Macaulay had written that, "Burgoyne was a man of wit, fashion and
honour and an agreeable dramatic writer and an officer whose courage was never ques-
tioned and whose skill was highly esteemed."

Edward Stanley was fair, not exactly good looking, but pleasing, with a determined
chin and was shorter than the average man. When he was twenty, having inherited large
sums of money from his mother, he took over the lease of The Oaks near Epsom from
his uncle, General Burgoyne. Annually he gave a house party for the races. This
arrangement must have suited his uncle who, in between leading a political life and a
military one, and now and again writing plays, was often out of England, often in debt
and never well off. In this same year, Edward gave parties during the season at his
house in Grosvenor Square. Horace Walpole, writing to the Countess of Ossory, on
30 April 1773, describes an evening spent in the Stanley's London house:

> I had the prudence not to stay for supper at Lord Stanley's. That festival was very

expensive, for it is the fashion now to make romances rather than balls. In the hall was a band of French horns and clarionets in the laced uniforms and feathers. The dome of the staircase was beautifully illuminated with coloured lights.

It was an astonishing age, both artistically and politically. Sheridan, Chippendale, the Adam brothers, David Garrick – names crowd the mind. Also the artists, including Reynolds, painted portraits of people who became ultimately famous.

In 1776, the General was no longer a young man, but King George III, who relied on his knowledge of the state of the military, had sent him to Boston to try to ascertain some idea of the current state of the Army. Charlotte's health was always a worry, and there is a scrap of a letter written by him just before he left England:

> ... to separate for any length of time, perhaps forever from the tenderest, the faith-fullest, the most aimable companion and friend that ever a man was blessed with, added severely to my anxieties.

He also wrote to the King:

> To recommend to your royal protection, Lady Charlotte Burgoyne, who at my death will have to combat the several calamities of life, a weak frame of body, very narrow circumstances and a heart replete with those agonies which follow the loss of an object it has long held so dear.

In June 1776, six weeks after he left England, Charlotte died. She was buried in Westminster Abbey.

Knowsley in 1832.

The following winter, General Burgoyne was back in London. He had been appalled by the state of the British Army and engrossed himself with plans of campaign in the American States, discussing nearly all his ideas with both the King and Lord North, the Prime Minister. Problems included a lack of troops, total mismanagement and general chaos in the armed forces.

Life in London, however, carried on as it had done for the last ten years. Only the King and his Prime Minister had serious worries.

Horace Walpole wrote to Sir Horace Mann on 18 June 1777:

> … one effect the American war has not had that it ought to have had; it has not brought us to our senses. Silly dissipation rather increases, and without an object… It is the fashion now to go to Ranelagh two hours after it is over… Lord Derby's cook lately gave him warning. The man owned he liked the place, but said he would be killed by dressing suppers at three in the morning.

General Burgoyne was a superb leader. He always dressed impeccably, travelling with numerous trunks of clothes. The soldiers adored him. He had something about him that the rough, illiterate men, who made up the English Army, respected, and it would not have been his fine lace and his airs and graces which won their admiration. 'Gentleman Johnny' had the advantage of having led various armies through different countries. He spoke several languages and his nickname was apt.

This story is not concerned with the implications of the American War of Independence, but only so far as it concerns General Burgoyne. In a fatal attempt to detach the colonists from Canada, he was surrounded at Saratoga by General Gates and the American army and forced to surrender with 3,500 men. A few months before this final surrender, men were deserting by the hundred and several thousand others were short of food, wounded and demoralised. The relief forces, which Burgoyne expected, had never arrived. He had addressed 400 American Indians who were part of his army, saying they were "not to use scalps, no killing of the wounded, no wholesale ravaging of the country."

At the time of his capitulation, Burgoyne agreed with the Americans an extraordinary document. He proposed that, "The British would be allowed all the honours of war and a free passage to Great Britain." His courage and dramatic irony never left him. Everything he did, he did in style, so that when he handed his sword over to General Gates on surrender, Gates, being so impressed by his enemy, handed it back. General Burgoyne's own regiment were sent to protect him on his way back to England. He had surrendered on 14 October 1777 and on the 17th the Convention of Saratoga came into effect.

General Burgoyne had every reason to wonder if he would get home safely. Like anyone else in his position, he wanted to explain his side of whatever report should arrive in England and let it be known he was still alive. A short note, written to his nieces on 20 October 1777 from Albany, a few miles from Saratoga and where, presumably, Burgoyne was a prisoner, still exists, although part is illegible:

I beg you to apply to Lord Derby… to have all the details of events sent to Hornby at Winwick.
Everything that is affectionate in particular to Hornby.*
    Your most affectionate Uncle,
        J Burgoyne.

In May 1778, his health deteriorating, General Burgoyne was back in England. Lord Derby did all he could to suppress the indignity which Burgoyne had to face on his return. However, having a fluent, strong and attractive personality, John was eventually able, with the help of his Whig friends, to regain his seat in Parliament when the Whigs returned to power in 1782. In time, he was made a Privy Councillor and Commander in Chief of Ireland.

It was whilst he was in Ireland aged nearly 60 that Burgoyne became romantically interested in the opera singer, Susan Caulfield, who became the mother of his three children. The first, a son, was born in August 1782 and was christened John Fox, at St Anne's Church, Soho. This son was destined to achieve great eminence, becoming a Field Marshal and attaining a Baronetcy. Susan also had two daughters, Maria and Harriet. Maria inherited her parents' love of music and was, in many ways, very like her father, who must have adored her. She had a cherubic, pretty face with light brown curls.

His father having died, Edward Stanley had become the 12th Earl of Derby. In April 1775, his wife Betty had given birth to a son, also called Edward, and they now planned an even more splendid celebration than ever before. It was to be a Venetian Regatta with twelve pairs of boats, which were to race from Westminster Bridge to London Bridge and return. There were barges decorated like the gondolas in Venice. However, bad weather prevented the race, so it was arranged that on the first bright day a flag would be flown from Westminster Bridge so that everyone could see it and the race would be held. On that first fine day large numbers of guests and hangers-on followed the course with shouts of amusement, no doubt 'huzzahing' their favourites.

However, this was probably the last great party that Edward, the new Lord Derby was to give. With the ennoblement and inheritance and the responsibilities they brought, he began to take part in the debates in the House of Lords, and gradually gave up his youthful follies. Although he did continue to gamble, it was Betty, with her love of whist and loo, and her obsession for gambling for high stakes, that very soon began to threaten their way of life.

Edward acted as steward at Epsom for the summer racing and asked parties of friends to stay with him at The Oaks. The Earls of Derby had always maintained a stud for breeding and the racing set included the Prince of Wales, 'Old Q' (the Duke of Queensbury) and Charles James Fox.

Edward and Betty, who were both in their early twenties, continued to entertain lavishly at Knowsley, where Burgoyne visited them and where he wrote several of his plays. Betty's spirits never flagged and her sudden jump from a window onto the grass

---

* 'Hornby' refers to the Revd G M Hornby, Rector of Winwick, the husband of Derby's sister Lucy, Burgoyne's niece.

Edward 12th Earl of Derby (1752-1834)

below when she saw some visitors arriving merely left her laughing.

There was an occasion when Lord and Lady Derby entertained friends at The Oaks for a cricket match, which was then the fashion. The Duke of Dorset was there – a Whig – and as Georgiana, Duchess of Devonshire wrote, "he was the most dangerous of men, great beauty, unaffected and simple and persuasive." The following day, all the ladies played cricket, as a joke. Betty was the most energetic and before long there were rumours that she was having an affair with the Duke of Dorset.

Betty had been presented to Queen Charlotte and an observant lady remarked that, "in spite of her beautiful costume and load of diamonds, she did not look so satisfied as the newly married Georgina, Duchess of Devonshire."

During the spring of 1779, there were also fears of a French invasion. Lord Derby, who was with his militia at Winchester, liked his personal comfort, so he had a stable and kitchen built. He slept in the tent his uncle, General Burgoyne, had used at Saratoga, and Betty organised parties to entertain the officers. They were last seen together on 2nd May at St James's Palace and a few days later, Lord Derby told her to leave his house.

"I hear Lord Derby is going to be divorced and that the Duke of Dorset is to marry her," wrote Princess Amelia to Lady Mary Coke. The Duke of Dorset confessed to Lord Derby, saying that he would marry her as soon as the law would allow. "Then, by God, I will not get a divorce," cried Lord Derby. It was said later that he burned her portrait at Knowsley.

Betty went to live on the continent and her three children were brought up at The Oaks and at Knowsley. It is questionable if they ever saw their mother again. The Duke of Dorset married someone else and 'The Maid of the Oaks' was no longer received by Queen Charlotte. Her mother and brother supported her and a few friends who were devoted to her continued to see her. When she returned to London from Lusanne, she spoke French so fluently that she was frequently taken for being French. Towards the end of her life, she was living with her brother in Scotland. She died in 1797.

In August 1792, General John Burgoyne died at his home in Hertford Street, Mayfair. In the *Gentleman's Magazine* for that month there is a summary of the events of his life and states "The regrets for his death will be extended and lasting."

Burgoyne requested a private funeral. Susan Caulfield, the mother of his illegitimate children, attended. She is then thought to have returned to Ireland. His last will and testament was seventeen pages long and in it he remembers "Dear Sue." He left her the substance of his estate with a reversion to her son. He left the diamond, which had been his wife's pride and given him by the Monarch of Portugal, to Lord Derby, and also requested that "my body be interred in the cloisters of Westminster Abbey as near as may be to the remains of my late inestimable wife, Lady Charlotte Burgoyne."

3

Lord Derby and Eliza Farren

In 1777 the manager of the Haymarket Theatre wrote that "her person is genteel and above the middle stature, her countenance full of sensibility and capable of expression, her voice clear. Miss Eliza Farren will be a valuable acquisition to our London theatre. We think she has genius." Before long she was acting with Mrs Jordan and Mrs Siddons at Drury Lane.

Eliza was one of the most admired actresses of the day and was at her best in comedy parts. When Horace Walpole saw her in General Burgoyne's play *Lady Emily* he considered it to be "one of the most finished of all her performances." She had beautiful eyes, portrayed in the portraits of her by Sir Thomas Lawrence and George Romney which show us the pleasing way in which she tilted her head, smiling. She only lacked sensuous curves. Charles James Fox was, at one time, rather taken by Elizabeth Farren, until he saw her in a breeches part. "Damn it! She has no prominence before or behind, all is a straight line from head to foot."

Eliza was kind and considerate, and like her contemporaries Mrs Kemble and Mrs Siddons, she always behaved like a lady. She lived with her mother, Mrs Farren, in Green Street, not far from Drury Lane. Lord Berwick, a well-known diplomat said in later years:

> Ah, those charming suppers at the bow-windowed house in Green Street, where I was admitted when I was a very young man and where one used to meet General Conway, Lady Ailesbury and the old Duchess of Leinster, General Burgoyne and all the pleasantest people in London.

And then he would usually end with eulogies on Eliza's acting in *The Heiress*, saying, "Ah! That game of chess, that game of chess. I shall never see anything like it again."

It was not surprising that Edward Stanley and his friends went to Mrs Farren's suppers. For at least ten years, the new Lord Derby had attended on Eliza, though there was no evidence that their friendship was anything more than platonic. However, as her fame as an actress grew, their courtship became the subject of gossip.

We now no longer hear of Lord Derby giving his extravagant parties. He appears to have spent part of each year at Knowsley and he always stayed at The Oaks in the autumn, where he kept a pack of hounds. He was in London during the season and he sat in the House of Lords. He had steadfastly refused to divorce his first wife, Betty.

In December 1789, Boswell recorded:

At coffee and tea were Miss Farren and her mother and Lord Derby. I was quite delighted with the English accent of Mrs Kemble and Miss Farren. Lord Derby was very pleasant, the attachment between him and Miss Farren as fine a thing as I have ever seen – truly virtuous – admiration on his part, respect on hers.

When Lord Derby's wife, Betty died on 14 March 1797, Eliza Farren was thirty-nine. Just over a month later, on 8 April, she took her last farewell on the stage at Drury Lane where she was playing Lady Teazle to a very appreciative audience. As the curtain came down for the last time, she burst into tears. Eliza never appeared on stage again, but her thoughtfulness and her natural elegance and dignified manner remained.

Miss Mellon said of Lord Derby, at the time of his second marriage:

Although he was forty-five, he had an excessively large head surmounting his small, spare figure, and wore his hair tied in a long, thin pigtail. This, and his attachment to short, nankeen gaiters, made him an easily recognised subject in the numerous caricatures of the day.

The couple were married by his brother in law, the Reverend G Hornby, the Rector of Winwick, and a reception was given by Queen Charlotte in honour of the bride. Eliza was presented at court on 11 May. "She was free from affectation and embarrassment and was simply dressed in white Chamberry gauze and white bugles and her head ornamented with a single small white feather and spray – her hair slightly powdered. The Countess went to court in the plain family coach attended by two footmen in their usual liveries. The whole appearance devoid of ostentation or parade – The Earl of Derby in mourning!"

Knowsley, Lord Derby's house, was vast, with superb views looking over the undulating Lancashire countryside towards the Mersey, with the already growing city of Liverpool in the distance. There were two Georgian wings, at right angles to each other and, facing the forecourt, were two round turrets. The 18th century sash windows and the warm colour of the red brick gave the house a pleasing and noble air. The wide carriage drive, sweeping up to the front of the house, was impressive and various roads, coming from distant parts of the park, wound through the woods.

Beyond the flower gardens and terraces, which were immense and produced flowers all year round for displays inside the house, were vegetable gardens and what must have been fields of potatoes. From the records of the time we know that labourers "washed the potatoes, mowed nettles, hoed vegetables, levelled rabbit holes and helped in the slaughter house", where hundreds of animals were killed. Ale was also brewed.

Several generations had altered and enlarged the house, and in Lord Derby's time alterations were needed because most of the bedrooms were 'passage rooms'. He had employed Robert Adam for work on his house in Grosvenor Square and The Oaks, but his plans for Knowsley were never carried out, perhaps because money was short, so much being squandered by him in his younger days.

Lord Derby's sister, Lucy Stanley, had married Geoffrey Hornby, who had inherited Winwick Hall from his father. Earlier in their marriage, her husband had frequently been away with his militia, so Lucy lived in part of the house at Knowsley with her eleven children. Winwick Rectory was in the gift of the Earls of Derby and was reputed to be the richest living in England. It was worth £7,000 a year, together with a large, comfortable house, only twelve miles from Knowsley. Frances, Lady Shelley, described life at Knowsley when she was staying at Winwick Hall with her Whig cousins:

> ...who had their father's talents and their mother's plain looks... There were no refinements of furniture in that old rambling house. There was a terrace where the ladies waved to the sportsmen and watched the arrival and departure of carriages, riding horses, etc.

The Hornby children were all under twenty at the time of Lord Derby's second marriage to Eliza Farren and a year previously, in 1796, the eldest son, Edmund Hornby, had married his first cousin, Charlotte Stanley, in the chapel at Knowsley. When all the Hornby children were at Knowsley, plus the three Stanleys – the children of Edward who was a young widower – the three children of Lord Derby's first wife, and the Burgoyne children, the total came to eighteen.

So with all these children, who must have shared the same nurseries and who were all using the chapel as a playroom, it is not surprising that romances developed. They were nearly all cousins, and the family trees show that the families were already becoming inextricably mixed and the generations overlapped. A fourth generation son and heir pleased old Lord Derby enormously, but all four eldest sons being called Edward make the task of writing any form of family history somewhat difficult. This tiresome fashion of the time whereby parents of every generation called their offspring after themselves, their brothers, sisters, aunts or uncles, parents or god-parents, means that there are numerous Edwards, Carolines, Charlottes and Susans throughout this story.

Whether Eliza had visited Knowsley before her marriage or not (and I am inclined to think she had), her first arrival as the new Countess, after a few weeks at The Oaks, must have been a daunting experience. She had, of course, been intimate with the kind of life and the way it was led in such houses, for instance when she had produced and organised the amateur theatricals for the Duke of Richmond, but to *live* in such an enormous house as Knowsley was another matter.

In London, Lord and Lady Derby mixed with playwrights and actors, but in the country they met with and entertained the local gentry. Somebody once said, "gentlemen had homes in the country and houses in London."

For Lord Derby and his second wife, life was extremely happy. They enjoyed the company of the numerous children, but as the house was so large, they need not have disturbed old Mrs Farren, Eliza's mother, who also lived there, as they ran about on the wooden floors. The house was usually full of visitors and during the season Lord Derby and Eliza went to London and to the Oaks for the hunting in the autumn.

George Hornby wrote of his memories of Knowsley when he lived there as a child:

> One has to remember that in so large a house the three or four different families

who lived in it were spread about so as to comfortably take up the entire house. Mrs Farren has a room near Eliza. People came and went so a visitor might not notice who arrived and left and it wasn't unusual to come across new faces unexpectedly.

George continues:

> Lord Derby after his second marriage was always very exact in looking into his affairs and scarce a morning passed that he did not go into the office before breakfast. Lady Derby once told me that when she had married they had only a clear £10,000 a year, so much was in lease of 99 years and so much debt to discharge. She was herself one of the most disinterested persons I ever knew and made his honour and happiness her chief consideration. I have pleasure in saying this because I well know it to be true.

Knowsley had been without a Countess and the complicated hierarchy of the upper and lower servants had to be considered, together with the grandeur of the housekeeper, Mrs Brown, who reigned supreme in the world below stairs. Also, having had no-one running the household meant that much of the work carried out by the servants had become slipshod and neglected. Attending to the enormous numbers of retainers and the vast amount of relations, who paid long visits, must have required considerable tact. Knowsley could house up to 30 or 40 guests at a time, together with their children and servants, their carriages and horses.

George Hornby wrote:

> To give you an idea of what passed at Knowsley in the early period of Lord Derby's first marriage, when he afterwards used to lament of his 'youthful follies', my father told me that on getting up one morning earlier than his wont, he went downstairs and, on passing through the Drawing Room, found the wax candles burning down to their sockets in the bright summer morning, and on coming to the waiting room, saw two tall footmen (in the red stockings they then wore) stretched out on the floor in a most profound sleep. Nobody regretted more than my uncle (Lord Derby) all his losses at play, sales of property and dissipation of his early life and one may say that his long acquaintance (without blemish or spot) of fourteen years with his second, incomparable wife, proved to be his salvation. In the dining room, we, the children, were made to drink the toast – "God bless the king and the good Earl of Derby."

Next to the breakfast room was the 'waiting room' where servants were always in waiting in the days when bells were scarce. George Hornby tells us:

> ...the furniture was rich satin. There was a dining room for the upper servants to which they all proceeded in great state, led by old Mrs Brown in full dress. Dear old 'Nanny Brown', housekeeper at Knowsley for 40 years and who had known it from childhood. Her portrait (younger and somewhat flattered) she bequeathed

to the house and it still hangs in the storeroom. She was the very model of a very aristocratic old housekeeper, about 50 when I first remember her, a vigilant dragon over servants and watchful over her master's interests, yet kind with all and particularly so to children. Her toilette about 1.00pm, presided over by the stillroom maid, was a thing to see and she issued forth with powdered head and cap of large dimensions, to conduct the procession of Ladies Maids to dinner at 2.00pm in great state. To see her in her progress through the sitting rooms, attended by Peter Gardener, the old carpenter, blind fixer etc., was to see the Nurse in *Romeo and Juliet* with her man 'Peter'.

Mrs Brown began her life at Knowsley as a stillroom maid, eventually being promoted to housekeeper. She said, "and here I have been girl and woman nearly 60 years." George Hornby tells us:

> This mention of 60 years which seemed to me, a child, an eternity, made me say '60 years!!!' 'Yes child, and do you know why I have been here so long?' to which, of course I said 'No, indeed I don't.' 'Well then,' (said she) 'little pitchers have long ears, and mind and remember what I tell you, it is because in all that time I have heard all and seen all and never said nothing, and let that be a lesson for you.'

George also tells us of a time when Mrs Brown had been showing the house to a party from Liverpool and, it seems, was little pleased with their remarks:

> And when they came to the Dining Room (said she) they turned up their noses and said they wondered Lord Derby had such a shabby sideboard, but I told them, 'Yes, I can suppose you Liverpool trades folk would have had a handsome piece of mahogany but a plain table with handsome Damask napkins over it does very well for my Lord,' and they had not a word more to say for themselves.

Judging by various letters written in later years, Eliza appears to have been universally popular. If she was criticised at first for being an actress, it was quickly forgotten, and being a person who acted unconsciously (as I think she did), the phrase 'an actress off the stage and a lady on it,' is apt. One of the first things she did on arriving at Knowsley was to stop the cock fighting in the drawing room. Another note states,

> She did, after her marriage, as far as it befitted her, continue to associate with... Mrs Kemble, Mrs Siddons and Charles Kemble who were always invited by her and the two former visited her at Knowsley, but she had admirable judgement and tact and never inflicted on Lord Derby the company of those who were not fit company for his table, even of her own relations, though she saw them and showed them every possible kindness. Her mother... lived with her and was the object of her most devoted, respectful and dutiful care. I have seen few such daughters! Indeed, to what relation of life was she not a model of excellence?

Eliza's first child, born in 1798, died, but during the following three years she gave

birth to Lucy, James and Mary Stanley. Some years earlier, Lord Derby had taken in
General John Burgoyne's children – John, Maria and Harriet Burgoyne. It was Maria
Burgoyne, who had grown up at Knowsley and was eighteen years old when Eliza had
her last baby, who became such a close friend – almost an adopted daughter. Maria's
sensitive feelings and understanding ways were in sharp contrast to Eliza's more robust
character. The gentle Maria was perhaps more genuine than the great actress.

In 1797, Maria was fourteen and Phipps Hornby (son of Geoffrey and Lucy Hornby)
who went to sea this year, was twelve. Maria was a warm-hearted, gentle creature,
who had inherited her father's charm, sympathy and understanding. She would have
known little of the fears of war. However, for Phipps, who quite likely had never been
on a ship before, homesickness, loneliness, fear and illness were almost a certainty,
though excitement made up for a lot.

Maria seems to have been Eliza's constant companion. They were both supremely
fond of 'keeping the family together', and when masquerades were performed, all ages
joined in, and it is likely that Maria undertook the musical side as she had inherited her
love of music from her mother, Susan Caulfield, which she passed onto her children
and grandchildren. Masquerades continued to be a favourite amusement:

> ...in the bustle and confusion of our masquerade... Our evening went off very
> well and the children were highly delighted. I think the characters were chiefly
> as follows: Lady Derby, an Irish washer woman, Georgina, Louisa (Hornby) and
> I three witches, Maria (Burgoyne) and George (Hornby) two excellent old fash-
> ioneds, James (Stanley) a friar, Fanny (Hornby) a Quaker, and afterwards dressed
> by Mrs Howis exactly like Brown, looking so like her (even without her mask) as
> quite to startle and alarm some of the servants. ...Edward (Stanley) a clown...
> Col. Burgoyne (Maria's brother) as Jack in the green... there was a variety of char-
> acters and I hardly know whether the children or servants were more amused, for
> I assure you there was a very large audience.
>
>   It was all over soon after eleven as was proper on Saturday night, but I have not
> even yet got my room to look like anything but Masquerade Warehouse as indeed
> it has done for some days for I had hard work providing dresses for all of our
> children and myself. I wish you could have been here, it would have pleased you
> to see how pretty all the children looked dancing... [illegible]... which most people
> did in their most becoming masquerade dresses and without masks.
>   ...I am obliged to quit you in haste as the dressing bell has rung a long while.
>   Ever you most affect. CMS (Charlotte Stanley) 13 May.

Clearly Lord Derby had mellowed with age. He seems to have lost his old, irresponsible
self, which was replaced by a more sensible one. Thomas Creevey was a constant visitor to the Derbys, both in London and at Knowsley and from him we can glimpse a
fragment of what life was like in the early years of the century. Charles Greville wrote
of him:

> Old Creevey is an extraordinary character. He married a widow (Mrs Ord); she
> had something, he had nothing. He got into Parliament, belonged to the Whigs,

displayed a good deal of shrewdness and humour… he has a great many acquaintances, a good constitution and extraordinary spirits. He possesses nothing but his clothes, no property of any sort. He leads a vagrant life, visiting a number of people who are delighted to have him and sometimes moving about to various places as fancy happens to direct and staying till he has spent what money he has in his pocket. He has no servants, no house, no auditors; he buys everything as he wants it at the place he is at; he has no ties upon him and has his time entirely at his own disposal and that of his friends. He is certainly a living proof that a man may be perfectly happy and exceedingly poor… I think he is the only man I know in society who possesses nothing.

Creevey's amusing chatter, reflected in his numerous letters, his sense of fun and love of scandal, made him an entertaining companion. His quick repartee and Eliza's sharp wit would have been good listening for those that were there to hear.

In 1806, Thomas Creevey wrote to Lord Ossulton from Knowsley:

The Prince [ie George Prince of Wales, later Prince Regent] comes here tomorrow and I have just been looking at a magnificent state bed Lord Derby has made to receive him, tho' he says he trusts it will not cost so much as £2,000, which the papers gave to it… Our party in the house consists of Lord and Lady Derby and Hornbys without end.

In September 1807 Lord Derby writes to Creevey:

Whilst you stay at Knowsley, we may hope for the pleasure of seeing McRoscoe and his son here to dinner. All days are the same to me and you know six is my dinner hour.

A note to Creevey from the 12th Earl of Derby in 1809 asks:

I should be particularly grateful to you if you could obtain for us any information of the fate of Captain Burgoyne. His sister is naturally very much alarmed for his safety, especially as she had had no letter since he marched for Portugal.

A letter dated 11 October 1809 is from Thomas Creevey to Mrs Creevey, who was at Brighton with her daughters:

We have all just returned from a visit to Knowsley where we found Lord Derby looking old but very well, and my Lady, though she was wrapped up with the mumps, was most gracious to me as well as in her inquiries after you. She condescended to tell me stories of Lady Mary being so anxious for me that she rode about Prescot and the neighbourhood in pink ribbons canvassing for me, with a crowd following her and shouting and as I afterwards met the little girl on horseback, I stopped her and found her mother's account quite true.

During the same month, Eliza's daughter, Lucy, died, aged ten, and in the following month, Creevey writes on 11 November:

> We dine at Lord Derby's, nobody but us. Lord Derby was excellent in every re-
> spect as he always is, and My Lady, still out of spirits for the loss of her child, but
> surpassing even in her depressed state all your hereditary nobility I have ever seen
> though she came from the stage to her title.

By the autumn of 1828 when Creevey had seen Lady Derby during her last illness, she was highly reluctant to part with Maria, now Mrs Phipps Hornby, who had always seemed like a daughter to her. Accordingly, the Hornbys made two or three further short visits to Knowsley during the next few months, finally spending the winter there and remaining until Lady Derby died in the spring of 1829. She left her body to be cut up by a great friend of hers "because she knew that he was interested in such things." Her husband survived her, but Creevey says, "Knowsley without Lady Derby is like a house with all the candles put out." On 1 November 1829, Creevey was visiting Knowsley and records:

> It is very agreeable being here, I mean principally on account of Lord Derby. I
> never saw the agreeableness as well as perspicuity of his understanding to such
> advantage. Lady Derby, with all her jokes, agreeableness and real fun, drove all
> natural subjects out of the field for Dramatic Piety and twaddle, and he followed
> her in everything so that he is now his own natural self again, reads the paper
> from beginning to end... And comments with the skill of a Master. Then he shows
> in his innocent, natural way much more for knowledge upon all subjects than I
> thought he possessed...

In the early 1830s and up to 1836, Edward Lear was a frequent visitor at Knowsley, having been invited there to paint pictures of the birds and animals in Lord Stanley's aviary and menagerie.

Edward Lear was a very tall man with a slight stoop, whose eyes were covered by a thick pair of spectacles. Both the children and the adults in the house soon discovered that he was a man who kept them amused with his lyrics, nonsense and fun. At one time old Lord Derby had asked why the children rushed away from the dining room before a meal was finished and it was explained that the attraction was Mr Lear who was so funny. From that day onwards Edward Lear would eat with the family instead of in the steward's dining room.

An entry in one of his letters, dated November 1829, reads:

> Lady Mary Wilton sent over yesterday from Knowsley to say that the locomotive
> machine was to be upon the railway at 12 o'clock. I had the satisfaction, for I
> can't call it pleasure, of taking a trip of five miles on it, which we did in just quar-
> ter of an hour, that is 20 miles per hour. The machine was really flying and it is
> impossible to divest yourself of the notion of instant death to all upon the least
> accident happening. It gave me a headache which has not left me yet.

In the early nineteenth century many changes were taking place. The cotton trade was booming, and collieries and canals were changing the face of a large part of the North of England. Meals and eating habits changed as coffee, sugar and spices poured into England from India and the East.

In 1830 when King George IV died and his brother, hitherto seldom seen in public and having lived the life of an almost impecunious country gentleman with his large illegitimate family, came to the throne, hardly anyone knew what the new King looked like. Lord Derby was likely to have known only too well of the last King's disreputable life and with the advent of the new 'Sailor King', as he was called, he may well have felt that the old days when the Whigs were in power and he frequented Brooks's and Drury Lane, were so different, so alien and remote. The Court was boring and Lord Derby, who Charles Grenville described as a shrewd and sagacious old man, would not have been in the least surprised when his grandson failed to get into Parliament at the previous year's election – the Whigs were out.

It had been a bad year altogether, for cholera had swept through the country and in the two previous winters the frosts were of unparalleled duration and severity, which meant that times were extremely lean for the farmer. The country was being churned up by the advent of the railways so the farmers and also the landlords were worried as to the effect that this was going to have. The railways were rapidly taking over from the coaches, which by now had reached such a precision of timing that they were always punctual. The railways were not. The whole network of the Royal Mail was disintegrating. The porters at the coach offices and the guard on the night coach could no longer supplement their pay by taking illicit game to the newly rich.

Gardening was becoming fashionable and, at Knowsley, Eliza had had many of the flowerbeds altered. She had also gardened herself. Repton and Capability Brown had landscaped parks and gardens for large country houses in such a way that they were becoming visually part of the landscape. In thousands of villages, charming small Georgian houses with attractive gardens were built and looked very much as they do today. Cottages had improved and the traditional cottage garden had begun.

4

Lina Denison

Caroline Hornby, always known as Lina, was the second daughter of Phipps Hornby and Maria Burgoyne. The family lived at Winwick Cottage, twelve miles from Knowsley, which both Phipps and Maria knew well from their childhood. In 1828, Lina was ten years old, and much of what we know about her and her life at this time is described in her journal.

> Next to our own dear house comes in my affection Winwick Hall, the house of my father's childhood, to which we were always consigned on the arrival of each new baby at the cottage, there to remain until my mother recovered. It was a great kindness of Uncle James [James Hornby was an older brother of Phipps] and Aunt Hester, in getting on in life themselves, with no young children of their own and quiet in their own tastes, in saddling themselves with the charge of five or six healthy children.
>
> Our clothes were very different then from what we wear now. We never wore a flannel petticoat until after we grew up. Frocks were of printed cotton in summer, for the morning with long sleeves, short waists and skirts to the ankles. We dressed for dinner, that is, for nursery midday dinner, and put on white frocks with short sleeves for the rest of the day. White frocks were worn on Sundays. Morning winter dress was of 'stuff', as it was called, looking like a coarse merino, generally of a dark blue colour.
>
> For outdoor wear in summer – brown Holland frock or blouse – sometimes worn over indoor frock, and sometimes, in hot weather, substituted for it. It was a comfortable garment which required no care, in which we could climb, garden and play to our heart's content. Outside the garden in the height of summer we had tippets of the same material as the frocks. Our bonnets were straw in summer and beaver in winter. Stockings were white all year round (worsted in winter, cotton in summer), buttoned boots for walking and a kind of clod-hopping shoes with clasps for garden work.
>
> In my earliest recollections, gentlemen wore black knee breeches and stockings in the evenings and I remember my mother lamenting when these were exchanged for the black trousers of modern times, which she thought gave a commonplace and 'undressed' air.
>
> The furniture of our house was simple and pretty. The drawing room was furnished with a pretty, small patterned chintz on a white ground, and a carpet light green with bunches of white flowers on it.
>
> We had some kind of tubs in the nursery in which we were washed every morn-

ing with an extra scrubbing on Saturday evenings. Winwick Hall must have been in advance of its age, for it possessed a bathroom – the only one I remember anywhere. I remember my mother ingeniously improvising a shower by standing on a chair and pouring a jug full of water through a colander on the recipient who stood upright in the tub below.

For lighting we had mould candles in the drawing room, tallow dips in the kitchen and rushlight in all the other rooms. Even Knowsley, the richest house of our acquaintance in those days, was only lighted by a profusion of wax candles in abundance. I remember too on a visit to London in our childhood, how much we admired the gas, then a novelty.

My mother and father dined at six o'clock; at Winwick Hall at half-past six and at Knowsley seven, which I imagine to have been the fashionable hour.

Our household consisted of four servants, nurse, nursery maid, cook and a man. The nursery maid and cook did the housework between them and, for a time, the washing also – getting up for that purpose at one o'clock every Monday morning. They may have had extra assistance on washing days.

Our house was a very pretty one, thanks to my father planting and my mother gardening. My father had planted much with his own hands, but we had a gardener. As time went on and the family grew up, a nursery governess and a housemaid were added and a new wing was added by dear Uncle James.

My mother was our principle teacher and under her tuition we learned to read early and to be fond of reading. For a short time, we had lessons in writing from the old parish clerk and, I think, my father sometimes superintended our sums. Perhaps our two first nursery governesses may have superintended our needlework and 'samplers' but they certainly were women of humble attainments and I do not remember to have learned anything from them. I fancy they were more wanted to superintend our wardrobes and our meals, now that we had left the actual nursery, than for teaching.

The first two nursery governesses were succeeded by a Swiss of rather more pretension, Mademoiselle [name illegible], under whom we learned French. Phipps, junior, before he went to school, used to go down every morning for a couple of hours to the Hall to learn Latin and Greek from Uncle James, and as I had a desire to learn these languages, I was allowed to accompany him twice a week, I think, and take short lesson, which I generally did sitting on dear Uncle's knee, while Phipps stood beside him. Phipps was considered sufficient escort for me on the way to the Hall, as most of it led through a quiet path through the plantations and the Harthill meadow, but my lessons were much shorter than his, so I used to set out alone on my return and be met on the way by the governess.

It seems to have been the general idea that all young ladies should learn music whatever their natural powers might be and the result was that there was a great deal of tedious strumming and, as my mother thought, a great waste of time. We were well supplied with storybooks. On Saturday mornings we were all admitted to a special bookcase each to choose two books for the ensuing week.

In the spring of 1828, the Hornby family was increasing rapidly. Maria was expecting their eighth child, so a new wing was being added to the cottage.

It was during the spring of 1828 that the new wing of the cottage was built, so as soon as my mother was recovered from the birth of Elisabeth, she and my father and the baby all came to the Hall where we remained the whole Spring till the work at the cottage was completed.

Clearly Maria and Phipps were delightful and kind parents. In the Autumn of 1828, as in the previous years, Phipps, Maria and all their children, Maria, Susan, Caroline (Lina), Phipps (junior), Lucy, Geoffrey and James, (their youngest daughter was not yet born), were staying at Knowsley.

We paid a long visit every autumn at Knowsley, where the most remarkable figure was that of Aunt Derby, but in our recollections an elderly lady, tall, graceful and dignified, who was very kind to us children as she had been to our parents before us. Uncle Derby was, I think, more infirm than his actual years warranted, having suffered from gout. These were our great uncle and great aunt, as you know. Uncle Stanley, Lord Derby's son, Edward Stanley, who was a widower, lived at Knowsley during the greater part of the year, though he and his children had a separate house in town.

Knowsley was a very hospitable house and there was a large gathering there every autumn of relations, friends and county acquaintances, and our visits there made a pleasant change in our yearly life. I remember there was some racing on the racecourse in the park. Our visits to Knowsley were much too long to allow of their being a continuous holiday, so the governess came there with us.

There were some brilliant exceptions to these uninteresting evenings when we 'sat up', as we termed it, and went into the drawing room. On these occasions there was almost always dancing, or round games, or something pleasant going on, and we enjoyed them extremely. Some of these evenings occurred on 'public days' which were a function belonging to Uncle Derby's duties as Lord Lieutenant of the County. These public days were announced beforehand and then he was 'at home' to anyone who chose to come. There was a large dinner, which must have been like a Lord Mayor's Banquet, calculated on the average number of guests expected, and dancing afterwards. We children used to get to the upper front windows to see the carriages arrive, before we dressed for the evening.

The crowning festival of our stay was the 12th September, Lord Derby's birthday. On coming down in the morning, one always saw fresh plants, and I suppose the most choice ones placed in the flower stands, and it was the custom for everyone to put on a new dress, and the old Lord used to claim the privilege of kissing all the ladies when they came up to offer their morning congratulations. It was, of course, a holiday for us children and, in the evening, there were fireworks on the lawn, dancing in the drawing room and the day finished by several of the drawing room party, among which we were always included, going down to join the servants dance in the laundry. We were allowed to sit up for some of the earlier dances.

The most extraordinary part of the Knowsley arrangements was that which concerned the chapel. I do not suppose that this was a consecrated building. It was an oblong room in the house, with round topped, rather chapel-looking windows and fitted up with pews and a high reading desk or pulpit at one end. Prayers were read in the chapel by Lord Derby every morning but for the rest of the day it was made the recognised playroom for the children. In fine weather, most of our daylight play hours were spent out of doors, but on wet days we romped in this chapel just as we pleased, fought with savages in our imaginary desert island, or played other games equally as noisy. I do remember Arthur Stanley, the future Dean of Westminster, riding astride in this chapel on three large hassocks, one on top of the other, and his sister Mary near him on a similar elevation, but riding sideways as became a lady. The remarkable thing was that I do not think this desecration at all lessoned our habitual reverence for holy places and things, but how it ever came to be allowed is a standing wonder to me. On Sundays the chapel resumed something more of its proper functions.

When we finished our Knowsley visit in the autumn of 1828, Aunt Derby, who was then in her last illness, was so unwilling to part with my mother, and so unhappy without her, that my mother returned, and went backwards and forwards for two or three short visits, but this did not answer. Aunt Derby did not like to part with her, and my mother did not like leaving us for any length of time, so it ended with us all being sent back to Knowsley where we remained throughout the winter and till Aunt Derby's death, which took place on 23 April 1829.

The year 1830 was an eventful one for us, for my father determined that my mother should have the pleasure of a visit to her relations and we three eldest children were to accompany her. We went to London, where we stayed partly in Lord Derby's house in Grosvenor Square, and partly in that of Lord Stanley in Upper Grosvenor Street. We went to Westminster Abbey and to St Paul's and to one or two Panoramas or sights of that sort, and we went one evening to a very pretty representation of Cinderella at Covent Garden.

From London we went to Portsmouth where Uncle Burgoyne [John Fox Burgoyne was Maria Hornby's (illegitimate) brother] was at that time Commanding Engineer. We stayed there about a week, went, of course, on board the old *Victory* and made a steam boat excursion to Ryde.

We finished our southern tour by a second visit to Henley, during which the chief thing I remember is hearing the bells toll in the town for the death of the King, George IV – this had been long expected. We were brought up in a spirit of loyalty and respect of the 'powers that be' and had probably heard as little as might be of the private history of the dying sovereign.

We reached home again on 2nd July and somewhat flat, it must be confessed, did the rest of the summer appear after all this novelty and excitement.

On 15th September that year occurred the opening of the first steam locomotive railway for passenger traffic, that between Liverpool and Manchester. The Duke of Wellington, then Prime Minister, came down to Liverpool for the occasion. The leading train, in which was the Duke of Wellington, was driven by George Stephenson himself.

In 1832, money was short so Phipps accepted the appointment as Captain Superintendent of the Naval Hospital at Plymouth. We were all very sad at leaving Winwick, which was let to 'the Aunts', Georgina, Frances and Louise, Phipps's unmarried sisters. The journey was made by sea, for it was cheaper than a long journey by coach, but by our standards, seems to have been extremely dangerous as well as adventurous. Great was the sorrow of leaving our dear old home.

In the course of the afternoon, we were soon boating up Stonehouse Creek on our way to the Naval Hospital which was to be our place of abode. My father said he saw all our faces lengthen as he pointed out our house standing square, staring and ugly on the bank of the Creek; a great contrast in point of beauty to the house we had left, but it was a good house and proved a happy home.

From the time of my brother James's birth, my mother had something amiss with her spine which prevented, to a great extent, her walking and obliged her to go out in a bath chair. She was an excellent sailor and so she could, during the summer afternoons, enjoy hours of wholesome sea air without fatigue, sailing in a large wherry that we had, out in the Sound or up the harbour.

In addition to the scenery there was, in those days, a tolerable amount of historic interest attached to the shipping in the harbour. There was the *Royal Sovereign* that had carried Lord Collingwood's flag at Trafalgar, there was the *Bellerophon* which had fought in all the great actions of the old war and was also the ship to which Napoleon Bonaparte finally surrendered when he had left France after the Battle of Waterloo, still to greater indignity turned into a convict hulk (for convicts still worked in the dockyards in those days) and with her name changed to *Captivity*!

One very interesting event of the year 1833 was the visit to Plymouth of the present Queen, then Princess Victoria, and her mother, the Duchess of Kent. Windham Hornby was the midshipman in command of her (the Admiral's boat) and to this day he boasts that he 'had had the Queen in his arms' for the position was still unsatisfactory and it required a good spring to get from the side of the ship into the boat. The Princess, who was the first to be brought down the side, was desired to jump and did so and Windham seeing what was about to happen, stood up in the boat and caught her in his arms so as to break the force of the jump and lower her gently to her seat in the stern of the boat. As he did so, he saw that she was crying! Truly, 'the girl was mother to the woman' and the Princess was showing something of the self command which has always distinguished the Queen. She was frightened, as she might well be, by the sudden commotion which she did not comprehend, but she showed no token of fright but those quiet tears.

Our first sight of our future Queen occurred a day or two later, when she and her mother paid a visit to the flagship and we boated into the harbour to watch their return. She was dressed in a pale grey silk frock and white drawn bonnet. I think that the court was at this time in mourning which prevented any variety of colours, for she wore the same dress when we were presented to her a few days ago.

On another day, the Duchess and the Princess were present at a luncheon at the Admiral's house at which my father, who was one of the guests, was seated next to Sir John Conroy, the Duchess's chief attendant. Presently Sir John said to my father, 'The Princess is learning her lesson now.' 'What do you mean?' asked my father. 'Watch her,' said Sir John, 'and you will see that she is looking quietly first at one person and then another, and the reason for that is the Duchess by and by will question her about all the guests – who was so-and-so, where did he sit?'

One sees at once how valuable this training is to a Royal personage and that it probably contributed in great measure to the remarkable power Her Majesty has always shown of recognising those she has once seen. In the course of her observation, the Princess espied the gold medal attached to my father's uniform. She knew its significance, for in those days these medals were only given to men who had commanded ships in a victorious action against a superior foe. The Princess wished to know in what action he had won the medal. It was for the Battle of Lissa.

Our personal introduction to the Princess occurred a few days later when she and the Duchess paid a visit to Mount Edgecombe and it had been intimated to my father that they wished to land at the Victualling Yard on their return. I can see now, in my mind's eye, my father in the aforesaid ugly uniform, cocked hat in hand, giving his arm to the Duchess and handing her up the steps from the boat. The Princess held on to her mother's arm on the other side. Presently the Duchess asked for us and we came forward and made curtseys. I was much struck with the grace of the Princess's answering curtsey. A group of sightseers had gathered and the Princess, looking up, gave them a special smile and curtsey, and altogether her manner was most pleasing.

In the summer of 1834, we went for a long visit to Lancashire. The expense of the journey both ways by post was not to be thought of, so it was decided that we should go by sea and only come back by land in the late autumn when the weather would not be propitious for sea-going. We spent our time in Lancashire between Knowsley, Winwick Hall and the Cottage, our dear Aunt's who had removed there after my grandmother's death, which took place early in the year of 1833. I cannot remember all the stages of our land journey back to Plymouth as well as I did those of our southward journey four years previously, I only know that it lasted four days.

These were, of course, still pre-Victorian times in attitudes and manners. A good deal of the eighteenth century spirit was still the norm, although beginning to give way to the more prim but emotionally unpredictable social temper of the age that was shortly to follow. Maria Hornby was at pains to assure her children (with a trace of what could now be seen as a typically nineteenth century insecurity) of the evils of gossip, to the extent of exhorting them to speak of 'things' and not of 'persons'.

I 'came out' in the Winter of 1835, so this seems a time for a description of the balls and dances of that period. The waltz I believe had made its appearance in England at the time of the visit of the Allied Sovereigns in 1814, but it was very slow in making its way. It was generally thought un-English and not quite in accordance with English ideas of propriety. By the time I came out, it had so far crept into vogue as to divide the dances at a ball with a quadrille, which to the introduction of a 'gallope', was the general order of proceedings at a ball. All the 'fast' girls danced it, and many who where not fast, but there was still a sufficient number of objections to save one from being at all unpleasantly conspicuous by declining it. My father and mother were among the objectors, and I confess that my own feeling was so decidedly with them, that it was no sacrifice to abstain, and though this decision cut us out of many dances, we still greatly enjoyed our balls. Quadrilles then were very different from what they became later on when they were merely walked through as a sort of rest from the more active round dances. On the contrary, they were danced with pretty steps to lively tunes. My chief enjoyment was in the country dances at which there came one or two at the end of the evening being generally 'Sir Roger' or the 'Boulanger'.

The year of 1837 was an eventful one. Geoff went to sea early in the year. He was only twelve years old, a year younger than is normal age, but an opening occurred for him in such a good ship that my father did not like him to miss it. The anxiety however, rather told on my mother's health and she was unwell all the spring, and so it was a great boon when we received the kind offer of Mr Bastard, a country gentleman in the neighbourhood, of the loan of his house at Bovisand for the summer. We spent a very pleasant summer there. We had a visit there from Mr Lear, with whom we had made acquaintance at Knowsley the year before, and he made what is called *A Book of Bovisand*, that is a portfolio of sketches, which I think must be at Littlegreen.

The great public event of this year was the death of King William IV and the accession of the present Queen. This took place on June 20th, but the news did not reach Plymouth until the following day, June 21st.

In the evening, we walked along Staddon Heights, the hill above Bovisand, to a point from where we could look down upon the town and up the harbour. From the town came the sound of the tolling of church bells, and in the harbour the ships had all been put into mourning, viz: the white line around their ports painted out so as to leave the whole bulk black. Their flags all half-mast high and the yards tipped this way and that into a slanting position so as to give the idea of distress and neglect. On the next day, the Queen was proclaimed at Plymouth, the day after her proclamation in London, and at the moment when the proclamation had been read by the Mayor, a signal was made to the ships who all squared their yards and fired a Royal salute, after which the yards were dropped again to their dangling and dolorous condition.

My father's next appointment was to the dockyard at Woolwich and thither we moved in the early spring of 1838. My mother's health continued very indifferent and she was advised to try a course of bathing and water drinking at Ems, then the best known of all the German watering places. This, of course, required much arrangement. My mother thought that Maria would make the most capable housekeeper and companion to my father during her absence and the lot of accompanying her abroad fell to Susan and myself, to our great delight.

Maria had had a painful back since the birth of James and a nervous, perhaps depressive illness. She was adored by all her family and relations.

The Queen's Coronation was to take place on June 28th and my mother, ill and nervous, resolved to take our passage to Antwerp that was to sail on the coronation day. On the strength of this we gave up all thoughts of the coronation and declined two or three offers of places both for the procession and the Abbey itself. The baths and water at Ems did my mother a great deal of good and we remained there till the beginning of August. I remember we stopped two or three days at Brussels and took a day at Waterloo.

It was during 1838, when Phipps was appointed to the Dockyard at Woolwich, that I first met William Denison, who was stationed there as a Royal Engineer. William, good looking and clever, was fourteen years older than me. He was born in 1804 and was the third son and third child of John Denison of Ossington in Northamptonshire, there being fourteen children in all. As a small child, he and his brother George, were sent to a boarding school where the conditions were appalling and the discipline harsh. They then went to Eton where they remembered to tip Dr Keate, the headmaster, ten shillings when they left. They then had a teacher at home, which they liked because they were able to hunt two days each week. Three of William's brothers won firsts in classics and another a double first. They were a clever family.

In 1819, William had joined the Royal Engineers. In 1827, he was in Canada working for the Ordnance Survey. In 1836, he came back to Woolwich where, in 1838, he met Lina. Within a short time they were engaged. Lina writes in her journal:

My own marriage took place in the late autumn. For some months after our marriage we lived in the same house on Woolwich Common that my dear William had occupied before, but his lease of it was to expire at the ensuing summer and he had bought the long lease of a piece of land in Wood Street, on which he was building a house. He afterwards thought that would not have been a wise measure in a pecuniary point of view, but for the present this new house, our future home, was a great subject of interest. Dear William's work lay in the dockyard, where he was an engineer officer in charge of the building works, so I used to go down most days to luncheon at my father's house, spend the afternoon there, and wait till William's work was done, when we walked home together. In these walks, we often made a digression to look at our new house, and one day when we do so, the clerk of work stepped up to us as we were entering the enclosure and said, "I congratulate you Sir," "Thank you," was the reply, "but why?" "The swallows Sir. They have begun to build in your new house!" and I understand that the congratulations had reference to an old saying that "there is peace in a house where the swallows build." The house, however, was barely finished by midsummer. I was expecting my confinement early in the autumn and my mother thought it would not be well to encounter that in the damp of an entirely new building, so it was settled that when our lease expired, we should come to the dockyards house for a long visit. There, in fact, we stayed for between three and four months. There our dear Mary was born, and it was not till well on in the autumn that we took up our abode in the "house where the swallows built." There we remained for nearly six years and there our next three children, Susan, Willy and Frank were born.

A letter written by Maria on the evening of her daughter Lina's wedding day, betrays her very natural feelings. Marriages, as well as births and deaths, meant in many ways far more than they do today, for then daughters were always at home until they married. A regular, organised life was led by all the family, with meals always at the same time and the same family customs always adhered to. Sundays had now become far more of a ritual than hitherto; everyone went to church as a matter of course. The Hornby girls – Maria, Lina, Susan, Lucy and Elizabeth – had different duties in the house, such as the making of jam, supervising the still room, washing the best china, writing long letters and visiting both the poor and their friends. On the whole, they enjoyed themselves.

Weddings brought with them the sorrow of parting, for when a daughter left home, things would never be quite the same again, and the near certainty of giving birth to numerous children carried hazards unknown today. The excitement and the enormous trousseau must have left a mother feeling sad.

However, this wedding seems to have been a very happy affair. A letter from Maria to Lina, just after the wedding states:

> After you left us, we all went to our own rooms and had our cry fairly out. Dear Papa came to my room and we had our little talk together; and Susan fairly forced herself on dear Maria and her winning ways and dear Maria's own exertions brought them down in less than an hour to my room to see if they could cheer me; and they did so, dear girls.
>
> In the evening the party we had asked arrived soon after eight and after tea the young people went downstairs and joined the servants in a dance in the dining room... They danced country dances and made up a quadrille with the best music I could give them. The drawing room party dispersed about eleven o'clock and Phipps followed, then all of us went downstairs and finding cake and wine about, we stopped the music and begged to propose the health of Mr and Mrs William Denison and the wish that there might be more weddings in the family. This was drunk with three times three but in their own characteristic way each of the servants adding a wish of their own. We then retired, meaning to go to our beds, but Jamie rushed up with the tidings that George was dancing a hornpipe so down we went again, Papa only going to bed exclaiming 'Hornpipe! I hope he won't hornpipe any more of my glasses.' Phipps asked Jane to dance, Wyndam followed with Lucy the housemaid. On asking her she said 'I'm not much of a dancer but I will do my best for Miss Caroline' and I must say if her love is to be estimated by her dancing you have good reason to be satisfied. He tore up, he tore down, Lucy nothing loath going all his paces, with a swing in the pousette that baffles all description. I assure you they were nearly the death of us all and the servants were all excessively amused that they fairly roared with laughter… the servants kept it up till four in the morning and we have received their united thanks for the pleasantest evening they have ever spent.
>
> We are all now settling down to the quiet regular habits of old. Maria has been making a quite new arrangement of her room so as to remove if possible the look of desolation your dear little empty bed gave it. She desires I tell you that when Lucy was dressing her yesterday she told her that she thought 'Miss Caroline looked the Hemblem of Hinnocence.'

Lina's journal continues:

> The chief public event of the year 1840 was the marriage of the Queen. Woolwich illuminated on the occasion and we, like others, put up a V & A in oil lamps over the front door. It was a windy night and our house was on the side of the street exposed to the wind, so several of our lamps were blown out. There was a great sprinkling of oil on our doorstep and altogether our illumination was not a great success and it was tantalising to see our opposite neighbours on the sheltered side of the street glimmering away to perfection.
>
> At the beginning of 1843, the end of my father's five year tenure of his dockyard appointment came, and he was appointed Captain General of the Coast Guard. This involved a residence in or near London, so he took Shrewsbury House on Shooter's Hill, a house that had a history, having once been the abode of Princess Charlotte, who resided there for a time with her governess. Shrewsbury House though further from us than the dockyard was still within reach of a walk. Often did we dine there and walk home on summer nights. On one of these occasions, we were overtaken by a thunderstorm and as we passed the barracks we found the sentry in the act of unfixing his bayonet, explaining in a sort of apology that he thought it was dangerous to have iron on him in a thunderstorm.

The second child of William and Lina was a daughter, Susan, born in 1841, later to become Susan Breeks. By 1845 they had five children and, in that year, after a short spell at the Dockyard at Portsmouth, William was offered the Governorship of Van Dieman's Land (Tasmania), which he accepted. The same year he was knighted for his work with the engineers.

5

Tasmania: Van Dieman's Land

On 13 October 1846, Sir William and Caroline (Lina) Denison, with their five small children, left England for Van Dieman's Land (Tasmania). They were lucky enough to get adequate accommodation on a new barque called *The Windermere*, a trader of 650 tons. The accommodation they needed was vast. Sir William had spent £2,000 out of his own pocket on equipping himself and his family for a three-month journey and a stay of several years in a remote country. They took with them a great deal of furniture, as well as glass, crockery, plate and china, pictures, books and prints. Three of their servants also went with them – Spreadborough, Lina's maid, the children's nurse, Rosalie, and their butler.

Mary and Susan Denison, the eldest children aged five and seven respectively, were too young to remember the journey, but for Sir William and Lina it must have been very memorable as, in those days, there was always danger attached to a long sea voyage. Clearly, William and Lina were fit and well. They may or may not have had a doctor on board, but one wonders how our generation would cope if we undertook such a journey. Also, going so far away and knowing they would not be home again for many years, must have meant a sad parting from their many relations and friends. In fact, it was to be twenty years before they saw England again.

Friday, 16 October 1846 – from Lina Denison to her mother, Maria:

Dearest M,
When I sent off my first postscript at Spithead on Tuesday, I could hardly have hoped to be well enough to begin my journal so soon. I wish I could report as favourably on the ship's progress as well as my own; but alas, the wind that promised so fair when we sailed on Tuesday, only continued so till that evening; then it fell calm, then blew a gale from the south west and now it is calm again; so that after having suffered a great deal, we are still exactly where we were on Tuesday evening dawdling about within sight of the Portland light, in company with a few other ships which are in the same predicament.

Sunday, 25 October:

Since last Sunday, I have not been well enough to write. We had a fearful gale... I think I shall never forget the impression of horror produced by the sound of the sea striking the ship, followed almost instantly by the terrible cry of 'Man Overboard'. Everything was done that could be done but it was no use.

Sir William tells us in his 'Memoirs' that when they reached Madeira they were able to go on shore and after the cramped conditions in which they had been living, this must have been a great relief. But, within 24 hours they set sail again.

Lina wrote to her mother on 1st November from Madeira:

> Our northern stars are fast descending in the sky and soon we shall have lost sight of them; the Great Bear is very low indeed. I confess that the idea of losing sight of the northern stars gives me quite a melancholy feeling; they seem to be the last links between us and England.

They finally reached their destination at the end of January 1847 after more than three months at sea and, after a few days in the doctor's house, they moved into Government House, Hobart Town, which was to be their home for the next eight years.

Van Dieman's Land is a little smaller than Ireland. The first white settlers came in 1803 from New South Wales. They exported sheep. By 1825 the population had increased and a Government was established. The Governor was autocratic, for although he had to obey orders from home, it took nine or ten months to get a reply from England. The law was represented by the Attorney General, the Church by the Bishop, and the Army by an officer commanding the two regiments.

At this time, convicts were no longer going to New South Wales, so Van Dieman's Land became the sole destination for criminals from England. The total population was 66,000 and, of those 29,000 were convicts. The Denisons must have seen the groups of convicts, chained together, working on the roads and also the large number of children of only twelve years old who had also been transported. Convicts were a source of cheap labour and some became servants.

The climate was similar to England. The country was beautiful, with hills and valleys and a rocky coast. Hobart town had many Georgian buildings built of honey coloured stone and brick. There were a few public buildings. Pears, apples and figs grew in the gardens, as well as daffodils and crocus.

On 27 January 1847 Lina Denison wrote in her journal:

> Yesterday we drove to the Government garden. I can hardly tell you how delighted I was with the drive; the domain itself is more like an English park than I could have conceived possible; and the trees, though they have not the varied beauty of English trees, still look much prettier when near than they do at a distance. The views from the domain are really beautiful. The harbour is so landlocked that it looks like a lake with beautiful wooded hills on the other side of it. We passed a spot where they had begun to build a new Government house, which was never finished; and, pleased as I am with the old house, I am afraid I half coveted this, from the beauty of the position and views. At length we arrived at the Government garden and what a sight was there! The profusion of fruit exceeded anything I have ever seen before; plums, pears, apples, figs, vegetables of all sorts, some English flowers and some very beautiful native shrubs. Amongst it all there was the bright green of an English walnut tree, loaded like everything else with fruit, and some very healthy young oaks. Altogether it would be thought

a delightful garden anywhere; and to us, just come off a very long sea journey, it seemed little short of paradise!

Government House, which overlooked the harbour, was like an English country house. It had a nursery, schoolroom and a ballroom for public functions. When it was filled with the Denison's pictures, books and ornaments, it must have looked very like a home in England. We can be sure that it was made as home-like as possible, which would help make up a little for being cut off from England, which has no parallel today.

Lina wrote in her journal on 23 February 1847:

> On Sunday we had what we had never experienced, the 'hot wind' and it is the most extraordinary thing I have ever felt. Our English ideas of heat prompt us to open all doors and windows but that would not at all do here, where the great essential is to keep every door and window shut. By dint of this precaution the house and the church were quite cool, but the moment you stirred out to get from one to the other you were met by a hot blast, totally unlike anything I have ever felt before. Once indeed, by stepping out of the cool schoolroom, so like that of a half heated oven, that for a moment I almost imagined that something must be on fire, but it was only that the hall door had been left half open.

On 5 March 1847 she noted:

> William and I went yesterday on board *The Anson*, a female convict hulk, all female prisoners go there on their first arrival and remain six months, after which, if they behave well they become pass holders and are allowed to hire themselves out as servants; it is a melancholy sight, some of them young girls of twelve, thirteen and fourteen. A great number of the poor factory girls come out here as prisoners.

One of the first things that Sir William did when he arrived in Van Dieman's Land was to advocate the abolition of convicts from England. This was very unpopular as convicts were a source of cheap labour. However, he got his way and six years later, from 1853, no more convicts arrived.

Engineering was always one of Sir William's great interests and, in those days, it was a useful knowledge for a Governor. Hunting, fishing and geology were his other interests, as well as collecting shells, of which he eventually possessed 7,000. He also read and collected books.

Before the Denisons arrived, balls were almost the only form of evening entertainment, so Lina introduced Tableaux Vivants, and for less formal occasions, Table Turning, which proved to be a great diversion, creating talk and laughter. No-one had seen a Christmas tree before and, being summer, the church on Christmas Day was decorated with lilies and jasmine. The Denisons gave a dinner on Christmas Day for all their farm labourers and their families and the Denison's children waited on them all, handing round the food.

The Gold Rush of 1852, which created such consternation, was the cause of a great many people spending all their newly gotten money and then having to face a life of poverty. Lina describes how this affected then all.

> Everyone rushes to the Gold diggings at Port Philip. No-one is left at the uphol-sterers to do the mending. Our washerwoman and kitchen maid and dairymaid have all gone. The Archdeacon was obliged to lay the cloth while his wife cooked the dinner, every servant having gone. The price of everything has gone up. The singing master has gone, as there are so few left to teach. Our own servants have gone out to help cases of sickness and Spreadborough is a great benefactress. Our house is full of visitors and women walk about in beautiful satin dresses, dragging them in the mud... men drink and there are cabs full of noisy people.

When they were tucked up in bed at night, did the children hear the loud laughter and the drunken oaths of the people as they arrived at the inn on the opposite side of the road from Government House? Did they see the ladies parading in their finery?

There was a family occasion which Susan and Mary, the eldest girls, and Willy would remember in years to come. That was the almost ceremonial opening of the English box (their mail), which Sir William described:

> I have often thought what a pretty subject for a picture might be made of the open-ing of the English Box. How it would speak to the feelings of those who had ever lived in foreign parts. With us, it is a regular family festival; if anyone is out of the way, the opening is postponed till they can be present; then all the children assemble from all the different parts of the house, even down to little James.

There was a day when 28 bags of mail arrived for the Denisons. The excitement was intense, but when it was opened it was found to have been full of newspapers. The dis-may must have been terrible. Although the news of deaths and births must have come this way too, and all the enormous parcels which had been ordered from England, for example, shoes for nine little pairs of feet "for we cannot get shoes here," wrote Lina, though most of their clothes were bought in Hobart Town.

Sir William and Lina both travelled to remote places, they opened and inspected schools and made suggestions for improvements, then went to visit them later to see if their suggestions had been carried out. During Sir William's time there, roads were constructed and schools built. He was administrator, engineer and philanthropist. It is surprising that Lina managed to accompany him on so many journeys as often as she did when, by 1854, her family numbered nine.

Lina describes their arrival in Launceston:

> We travelled with our carriage rocking and shaking to its centre, William with his hat off acknowledging the cheers, looked anxiously forward ejaculating his old exclamation 'By the Lord Harry we shall overturn...' However, all was well and we reached home safely.

On 26 May, Lina wrote:

> We are amused this morning by seeing the departure from this Inn where we are staying of a couple who had come down from Hamilton to our ball on Monday. This morning we saw them set out, both on horseback; the lady with a sort of bundle, containing I suppose her ball finery, hanging at the pommel of the saddle; the gentleman with a little knapsack strapped to his. This is the way that everyone must travel in winter, to and from these out-of-the way places; as all except for a few great roads are impassable in winter for carriages.

After their various journeys across the island, the Denisons were always given a great welcome on their return to Government House. Lina's journal describes a time when William returned to Government House: "the children watched out of the window where they could see the harbour with all the ships decorated with flags... the streets were crowded, the shops shut and I was out on the veranda to meet the cavalcade."

We can begin to see the kind of life they were leading. There are large gaps, the picture is only sketched in, but we can imagine that it was a happy home.

22 January 1854, from Lina's journal:

> On Friday afternoon I walked along the beach with some of the children, to a favourite rock of ours because the waves beat up against it so finely; just as we had reached it we saw a man coming along the beach to meet us, whom we soon perceived to be one of the soldiers on guard at the Nick for he had military trousers on but a rough blue blouse over them instead of his uniform which gave him a very nondescript appearance. He made a sort of half pause as he passed me as though inclined to speak but then thought better of it and went on; however I soon saw him stop and speak to Mary, who had lingered a few yards behind to pick up some shells, she then came up and told me that it was not very safe to be out along the shore here today because there is a bolter out!
>
> I guessed what this meant, but being anxious to hear more we turned back and soon overtook the man who was loitering slowly along and peeping up into every ravine that came down to the shore; and then I asked him if there was an escaped convict anywhere in the neighbourhood: 'Yes, and it was pretty certain that the time that had passed since his escape, that he would reach the Neck tonight if he was not caught before.'
>
> 'And are you sent here to watch for him?' I asked.
>
> 'No Ma'am,' said the man with a naivety which rather amused me, 'I am only here for my own interest, you see, because we get a reward of two pounds if we apprehend him, but they are so desperate sometimes.' I did not exactly see after all what danger the children or I had to apprehend from a man whose interest it would so evidently be to avoid our observation. However as I saw that my friend had a pistol in his hand I concluded that he anticipated a fray and thinking it desirable to be out of the way of that, at all events, I thanked him for his information and hastened home with the children.

Under these circumstances, Lina appeared extremely calm.

Maria Hornby would have written to her daughter every week perhaps. The following letter provides some common sense advice and a picture of the Victorian attitude to bringing up children. Lady Hornby wrote to Lina:

> Do you, my darling, avoid my errors and watch anxiously the development of your children's characters so as not only to habituate them early to bear their respective burdens cheerfully but to exercise themselves so as to promptly make up their minds as to the best mode of lightening them. A cold or a little sprain or something happens to keep them in the house when they are longing to be out; instead of fretting over the trail teach them at once to turn their minds with gratitude to the numberless resources they are blessed with in their books, pencils, pens, etc. But under every circumstance, dearest, watch and see that they do not get listless habits; the lolling and rolling about with a book in their hands is destruction of energy; let them read as much as they please but not till they are so weary that they do not know how to sit or lie quietly. See that even to dolls and playthings, neat habits are practiced by the children themselves, not left to the school-room maid. I should now, too let the little girls begin to assist each other in dressing and undressing; it will help to make them independent.
>
> How does dear little Mary's work get on? I am glad that she has begun to mark, for when once that stitch is learnt the amusement is inexhaustible, such as working kettle holders for her friends. You must begin now on making the little girls dependent on themselves and on each other for amusement or you will become a slave to them. I was many years learning this secret for I assure you there is no tyranny like that of children over the mother who is always at their call for amusement.
>
> Your letter is full of the most interesting details to me, containing as it does, so much about your dear children which I was most anxious to know.

On 18 September 1854, Lina wrote:

> Now, my own dearest Mummy, I have time (which I had not yesterday) to sit down and have a comfortable talk with you on the subject of which my thoughts have been full ever since last Saturday, the eventful day which brought us the news of our appointment to New South Wales. I have never allowed myself to dwell much on the hope of returning home at the end of our term of service in this country; and I think too that if we had not taken up this colonial line of life, but had continued in the direct line of W's profession, we might equally have been abroad, equally separated from you and from our boys without any of the comforts and agreeableness of our current position. And now as to the honour of the thing for dearest William it is certainly a very great appointment for so young a Governor. Our friends and supporters here are in a state of great excitement.

Sir William and Lina were both much affected when they left Van Dieman's Land. They had made a great many friends and most of them they would never see again. After her last Levee, Lina tells us that she went up to her room and had a regular good cry.

Lina wrote in her journal on 11 January 1855:

> The last two days have been spent in an unceasing bustle in packing, arranging, taking leave of people, and I was really glad yesterday to have too much to do and not to be able to dwell on the thought of it being the last day in the dear old house which has been such a happy home to us now for nearly eight years. We have to leave it during the afternoon to make room for the sale (which is to take place today) of what furniture, etc. we leave behind.

The two boys, Frank and Willy, were sent back to England to live with Lina's parents – now Admiral Sir Phipps and Lady Hornby – who lived at Little Green near Portsmouth. Lina describes their departure:

> As well as hearing 'Three Cheers for Sir William and Lady Denison,' there were 'Three Cheers for the children' and then 'Three Cheers for the native born' and guns fired. Three steamers sped after us for twelve miles and then we heard them singing *Auld Lang Syne* and they produced glasses and drank our health and threw their glasses into the sea!

6

Sydney

When the Denisons arrived in Sydney, the capital of New South Wales, in 1855, the town stretched for two miles along the coast. It was a handsome town with early 19th century houses built of local free stone and often ornamented with iron balconies which had been sent out from England. The main street was always bustling with people, most of who looked, and often were, English. There were omnibuses, wagons, cabs, carts and carriages. There were inns with swinging signboards just like England. There were a few large public buildings and a new Government House which was built in the Tudor style. There were well laid out parks, a theatre, warehouses and, on the edge of the town, villas with gardens. In fact, it was very much like an English seaside town.

One of the most Australian things about Sydney was the number of large drays often seen in the streets. These were wagons without sides so that they could be piled high with loads of food, stores, etc. They usually belonged to sheep farmers who lived great distances away, often far from other people, and came into Sydney to stock up with everything, such as food, medicines and household furnishings. These goods were loaded onto the drays and a fine sight it was to see the whole family setting off home again. They would have brought with them produce, wool and leather to sell in Sydney.

These sheep farmers were tough people. Many of them would have been emigrants from England, who came out to Australia without much money, but with plenty of enthusiasm. When they arrived in the country, they would buy a piece of land, fence it and build a wooden house, perhaps only with the offer of help of one employee. They would then buy sheep, horses, bullocks, wagons and drays, and finally they would have built a store at the rear of the house large enough to hold all their supplies for weeks ahead. This store would be kept locked because of the threat of the supplies being stolen by bushrangers, usually ex-convicts, who roamed the countryside and lived as best they could.

Australia was a new and exciting country, but as in Van Dieman's Land, everyone and everything was affected by the gold digging, which had begun a few years previously, in 1851. The only restriction to digging for gold was a monthly fee of 30 shillings paid to the Government for a licence, which was granted to all who applied. A spade, crowbar, pick and a tent were all they needed and at night the fires outside the tents could be seen from miles away. By day every available vehicle was used from a bullock dray to a wheelbarrow. The successful gold diggers frequented the local inns, got drunk and squandered their earnings. 'Easy come, easy go' was the maxim, but it caused the more sober minded citizens to fear for the Colony's welfare. The knowledge of the gold diggings had a disastrous effect on sailors, farmers and many others, according to observers in 1853.

Lina Denison wrote:

It is impossible to convey an adequate idea of the impressions this astounding intelligence had upon the ship's company, crew and passengers. A kind of hysterical affection seized every man and woman on board. The only serious man left was the Captain, who had been informed by the pilot that the sailors were running away from the ships in harbour so that one and a half of them had been deserted by their crews – sailors refusing twenty pounds a month for the run to England in the wool ships, which now left the harbour with freights of gold equal in value to their usual cargoes of tallow and wool.

Later, she wrote:

I wish I could give you an idea of the extraordinary state these Colonies are in, in consequence of the astounding discoveries of gold at Port Philip. California seems a mere nothing to it. The gold is to be picked up in abundance close to the surface of the ground. It is sometimes even seen glittering amongst the grass. Those who left this place a few weeks ago to try their fortunes are already in possession of seven, eight, nine, or eleven hundred pounds, and in Melbourne people are so reckless of their money that a man goes into a shop, buys something which is, perhaps, worth 30 shillings, throws down a five pound note and refuses to take his change!

About three weeks ago I broke the little gold chain to which my eyeglass is chained and it never was mended to this day.

This house is really a fine one, Elizabethan in style and very handsome within. The individual rooms are all good and some of them beautiful, but it is a badly laid out house and the consequence is that there is not nearly so much room in it as you would imagine from its apparent size. My bedroom is the most perfectly delightful room you can imagine. Another charming room is the one I am now sitting in. It is what has hitherto been known as the private drawing room. There are large public rooms downstairs, dining room, ante room, drawing room and ballroom all opening into one another, but this upstairs room has always been the home room and when it gets our books and prints into it and about it, it promises to be almost perfection.

To Susan and Mary Denison, Sydney must have been exciting for it was the first town of any size the children had ever seen. However, in general far more attention was paid to official protocol in Sydney than had been the case in Hobart Town. Lina notes that on their arrival, the judiciary formally requested to be presented to her and appeared in full regalia, which took her somewhat by surprise. Part of her daily timetable was to be available from two o'clock until half past four each afternoon to receive visitors.

At the same time, Sir William was writing:

Railways are adopting the air of an English one, looking just the same. It is quite refreshing to hear the whistle and the guards calling out the names of the station, it sounds so homelike... It is a hopeless country to try and move about in and it is a standing wonder to me that this, which is so much the older country (colony), should be so far behind Van Dieman's Land as in this respect it is. There we had good roads to all the principal places and very tidy inns. Here there is hardly anything that is worthy of the name of road and the so-called inns hardly deserve to be ranked as public houses.

The so-called roads in Australia were appalling. At best they were often only tracks, not always easy to see in the dust of the dry season, and in the wet weather they were deep with mud.

Lina Denison describes their first journey inland, which makes it evident that for the Governor's family, travelling conditions were not easy:

It rained so hard we had doubts whether we should start at all. We set off in a close carriage. Met at the station by two gentlemen just come down from the country who told us that if we were going on at all, we had better go at once, for the roads were likely to be better now than in three hours hence. We had 29 miles to go with our own horses. From thence, William and the girls, Susan and Mary, with the aide-de-camp were to ride, leaving me with Nurse and baby (George), then only a few months old, in the carriage. Soon, a tremendous storm and the road became like a ploughed field and the uncomfortable thought of this ford still looming in the distance. The riders had, by this time, gone too far ahead for me to call the girls into the carriage.

At about six, drivers and riders met at the point where we were to turn off to the farm but were informed by a man that crossing the ford was out of the question! He had had difficulty in getting over half an hour ago and the river had been rising rapidly ever since. Sunset and darkness approaching, here was a state of things: horses tired, riders drenched, roads changing from ploughed fields into marsh, baby begging to be fed, fretful, hungry, and to crown all our baggage had vanished!

To reach our destination was impossible. We had nearly resolved to ask shelter from Mrs Cooper whose house was not far off. She would have contrived to take us in somehow being quite used to casualties in this country of bad roads and no bridges. Just imagine, Governor and Governor's wife, two daughters, a baby and nurse, aide-de-camp and two man servants, two orderlies and eight horses all coming to be housed at a moment's notice, on a family which I believe is numerous. So, it was decided to push on. Those four miles were worse than all the rest.

By and by, I heard the coachman call out, "Tell me George, how am I to get through this?" I looked out and saw that 'this' was a regular pond. The answer was inaudible. We struggled though with jolting and sinking to one side.

A scream from Nurse, then on for a mile, and then, "George, have you any idea where we are?" However, we made on. If the horses should come to a standstill with poor baby and all... However, we came to an Inn and joy upon joy there was W and our baggage there also. So, we had dry clothing and I made the girls go to bed and nursed them up with tea and they are none the worse.

In the dry season, there was always the fear of drought and it was essential to carry enough water for the journey. Acres of land would become dry and parched and it was unwise to endlessly look for a creek which had a little water. Creeks were riverbeds, often with perpendicular sides and they were extremely difficult to cross. Everyone hoped there would be tracks to follow from a previous wagon which had already crossed over.

Sir William's main frustration with New South Wales seems to have been that here he was much less his own master than he had been in Van Dieman's Land. By 1860 he had had five sets of official advisers in just over three years, without a single satisfactory piece of legislation being passed. His personal influence had been directed mainly towards reorganising existing convict labour so as to provide sufficient work for all and securing efficient defences, particularly of Port Jackson, the port of Sydney. The Denisons' feelings of exasperation with official obstruction must have been communicated by Lina in a letter to her mother, for Maria comments in one of her letters back:

> Well do I know what it is to have one's husband checked, thwarted and abused and blamed instead of being supported in honest discharge of his duty. I have however learnt that a wife's duty is to control as much as is possible of her honest indignation, and at such times conduct and sympathise she must, but in the affectionate warmth of a woman's nature we are apt, at least I know I have been, to express more of indignation and irritability than is consistent with Christian forbearance, and I have always found that I have done myself harm, and my husband no good. So dearest, you will benefit from your mother's experience!

The Denisons were keen promoters of the arts and Government House was frequently a meeting place for artists and musicians. On at least one recorded occasion, the house was the scene of a 'Punch and Judy' show by the first Punch ever to come to Australia from England. However, the officialdom continued to frustrate them and in 1856 Lina writes of the difficulties in trying to make the arrangements for the formal opening of Parliament, recording that "A…. is a great man for forms and etiquettes." She also writes:

> …On Sunday we <u>drove</u> to church, it being the opinion of those who know the Church that is was too far to walk. I do not think so, indeed, we did walk there in the evening, certainly without the slightest fatigue.

In this last connection, Sir William occasionally reveals an engagingly innocent side to his character:

> I limped slowly down to the Chapel, being still in pain from my sprain, which was the result of an attempt on my part to show the midshipman on board the *Iris*

how to skip with two people holding the rope. When a man weighs upwards of thirteen stone, he has no business to make experiments on the strength of his tendons.

The picture conjured up of Sir William injuring himself demonstrating the use of a skipping rope is in character with that of him a year or so previously, rousing his family and guests to a fever-pitch of excitement over the fall of Sebastopol. On 11 December 1855, Lina describes how they heard the news, which had taken three months to reach Australia:

> We heard firing of guns, and looking out we saw the Mail Steamer from Melbourne coming in, all decked out with flags, people collected – then cheers. Then came a paper, sent by the Captain of the steamer with the news of the fall of Sebastopol. My good man (Lina constantly referred to her husband in this way) ran about the house rousing everyone. The girls sang over and over again *God Save the Queen* while they were dressing... Such joyous excitement, that it ended with us sitting down by the fire when evening came and rather wishing that such delightful news would not come on a Sunday, for happy though the excitement has been, the fact of its being so exciting had well nigh destroyed the peculiar Sunday comfort.

Unfortunately, the children are rarely mentioned by Sir William and Lina in their letters or diaries. When we do hear of them, they are referred to collectively as 'the girls' (Mary and Susan) or 'the younger children'. By 1858 we hear no more of Mary (it is known she died young) and Susan alone seems to have spent most of her time with her parents and accompanied them on some of their travels, the 'younger ones' being still in the nursery or schoolroom.

We can only guess at the kind of life Susan led. She appears to have enjoyed riding, sketching, and attending concerts, being musical like the rest of her family. She was like her father, as was her sister, Lucy, and both grew into very managing women! Lucy, or Mouse as she was nicknamed, was almost a midget, being a little over four feet tall. Her brother, Henry, was an accomplished organist by the age of eight and a piano was built especially for him so that his feet could reach the pedals. There is little to tell us more about the children, until they grew up, when nearly all of them were talented, plain like Lina, and musical. There were now eleven children, Alfred, the youngest, was born in 1857 and by 1860 Lina was pregnant again. She wrote to her mother:

> You cannot think how often our thoughts turn towards England now when William's time here may be drawing to its close, and how earnestly we pray that there may be a happy meeting in store for us.

It was fourteen years since they had left England so it was reasonable to suppose that they would return home when their time in New South Wales was at an end. However Sir William wrote in a letter to his mother in November of the same year:

The mail has made a marked change to everything relating to our future prospects. It brought me out a letter from Sir Charles Wood (Secretary of State for India) in which, acting upon the assumption that I would go wherever ordered, he requested me to proceed to Madras, where I should find my commission waiting for me. As you may imagine, the news brought with it much serious thought and much consultation between Lina and myself. There was, however, no doubt or hesitation as to our acceptance of the offer.

...My present idea is to move off bag and baggage by the January mail steamer, provided Lina is in a good enough state to travel. I hope and trust that all will go well with her and that she may be able to go on board without any risk... We suppose ourselves landed at Madras by the end of February. I shall not let those (children) who are to go home stay too long there, but pack them off after a very short delay; just enough to allow them time to give you an idea of the place. I think you may reckon on their arrival sometime in May.

Our packing will be formidable... I fancy few Governors move round the world with a library of 2,000 books and thousands of shells.

After the usual sad partings, the ponderous move took place.

7

Madras

In February 1861, the Denisons arrived at Port St George, Madras. Lina described their arrival:

> The next morning, Friday, we went on board the Government steamer, which was clean and comfortable but slow, and we arrived here just before daylight on Monday morning. The time of arrival had been pre-arranged and calculated upon as well as might be because all the authorities, troops, etc. were to be out to meet William, and they could not well turn out, nor could we land, during the heat of the day.
>
> Almost as soon as it was light, our landing had to be effected and it was, in itself, a novel and curious sight. Some of the members of William's new staff came on board and carried him off in a large boat, manned by native rowers, whose dress was a sort of white shift, bordered with blue, and slightly fastened in at the waist, leaving the legs and arms bare. The big boat was attended by four catamarans, each propelled by two, nearly naked, natives. These are supposed to be in attendance in case the big boat should overturn in the surf, for there is no pier or landing place and one has to come on the shore where the surf is sometimes very high. As soon as William had landed, he was received in form and drove off, surrounded by his bodyguard, to the Fort to be sworn in, a salute being fired from the Fort as he landed, and another as soon as he had taken the oaths.
>
> Then the big boat came back for us. The rowers sang a sort of monotonous song as they pulled. As soon as they got into the surf, down rushed a crowd of swarthy, almost naked figures, some to seize on the boat and drag it through the surf, some carrying chairs supported on poles which we mounted, one on each, and were carried through the surf and sand to where carriages were waiting for us, umbrellas being held over our heads all the while, for the sun was up by that time and was already getting very hot.
>
> Then we drove away to Government House in Madras, our town house, where we breakfasted and remained during the day, and in the cool of the evening, drove out to this place, our country house about five miles from Madras, called Guindy, where for the present, we remain.

From the earliest days of British rule in India, the idea had been firmly entrenched of making every English settlement, as far as possible, an exact replica of a fashionable town at home. The British presence had to impress, and so the classical style of domestic architecture was imported bodily, the veranda surrounding each storey being suitably modified to display the grandeur of the Ionic columns to maximum effect. Government House in Calcutta, for example, had a dining room occupying the entire centre of the house, approximately sixty feet wide and more than a hundred long, paved, like the drawing room, with grey marble, and with two great rows of columns to support the upper floor containing the ballroom.

Like Sydney, Madras was exposed and liable to frequent storms, but there any resemblance ceased. In Madras the bright, vivid colours and textures of both buildings and costumes alike, combined with the mingled aromas of different spices, was a novel experience for any European.

Lina's portrayal continues:

> …no pen or ink description could really do justice to the servants, with their very picturesque appearance, and very strange ways and habits. The swarms of footmen and butlers formed quite a spectacle when we arrived here, as they stood in two rows on the doorstep in their white dresses and turbans and scarlet and gold scarves to welcome us. All the male servants, belonging to both house and garden, are paid for by Government and so are also one or two dreadful harridans who make the beds. Altogether there are two hundred and fifty who are paid for by Government. In fact, each man does so little in India that it is necessary to have a great many to get through the work. Moreover, the servants get their own board and lodging. This is simple enough for a good many of them who sleep about on mats in the passages and on the verandas, so, as you go to your room at night, you pass along a sort of avenue of sleeping figures, with their turbans off lying beside them, but otherwise dressed much the same as by day. The stable servants we pay ourselves and so we do two ayahs who have been hired to assist in the nursery…

Shortly after their arrival in Madras, William gives an account of his average day at Guindy:

> Our life is rather peculiar. We get up in the dark, about five, throw on some clothes, and sally out for a walk or a ride, come in not later than half past seven, wash, have a bath and get dressed, read or write till half past nine, when we have prayers and breakfast, sit at home working under a punkah [a suspended fan] till half past four, ride or drive till seven, dine at eight and leave the drawing room about ten or half past.

William was similarly impressed by the grandeur and elaborate attention which surrounded them. He relates:

> Each bedroom has a dressing room and bathroom attached to it. There are no bells, but all you have to do is call 'peon' and a man is at your side at once. There are men, too, always at hand night and day to work the punkahs – a broad sort of fan, hung from the ceiling, which moves backwards and forwards creating a pleasant current of air. When we drive, the two horse keepers run one on each side of the carriage; when I ride, the horse's servant (or rather one of them, because each

horse has a man and a maid to wait on him) runs after me. I cannot venture into the garden or park but a man is sure to see me and rush after me with an umbrella. All this, to me, is rather a bore but I suppose I shall get used to it.

...no sooner do I open my door than up start four or five men in scarlet dresses who are waiting my commands and if I move about the house one of them is sure to follow me. Poor Lord Elgin said he felt like what he could imagine a lunatic would feel with his keeper always close to him.

Lina continues:

…I went into Madras for my first reception. This was a much more formal affair than in Sydney. There I merely announced in the papers what days I would receive and at what hours and they came in like ordinary visitors. Here it is in the evening, so everybody was in full evening dress and each person was formally marched up the room by an aide-de-camp and introduced as I sat at the upper end of it. It was terribly stiff, formal work and poor William groaned over it *sotto voce* whenever he could.

However, William and Lina's 'public breakfasts' (in Madras to begin with, but subsequently at Guindy), reminded Lina pleasantly of the 'public days' at Knowsley in her childhood, when she and her brothers, sisters and cousins had stood at upper windows and watched the numerous carriages as they arrived. The Indian carriages, however, were equipped with Venetian blinds and white covers to screen off the sun, and the dark faced, bare legged horse keepers were, as she explains, "very unlike English footmen.".

Soon after arriving in Madras, William came to realise the extent of the crowding and lack of sanitation in the city, and also the effect of the hot climate, on both the Indians and on himself and his family. He, therefore, moved the Governor's main residence permanently out of Madras to Guindy, leaving the town house for public offices. He later took the opportunity that arose to buy Bishopsdown, the house of the late Bishop of the Nilagiris, at Ootacamund, the famous hill station. He communicates his plans and observations in a letter to his sister-in-law, Charlotte Denison, in March 1861. By this time, Lina had left India for a few months stay in England.

I had no idea how closely these people pack themselves till yesterday when Susan and I, in our morning walk, passed through a portion of the town just in the rear of Government House. This was a mass of low huts, six feet high to the eaves. The lanes were twelve feet wide and the houses as close as they could pack. There is no fall to carry off the drainage or water to flush the gutters, and my only wonder is that fever and cholera do not sweep away thousands and tens of thousands annually…

By the time you get this, Lina will have arrived in England with five of the children. I put her on board the steamer on the 21st, but had I anticipated the bitterness of the parting, I should, I think have hesitated to accept the appointment of Governor. It is the great penalty attached to service in India that it breaks up all family ties, it separates husband and wife, and always parents and children.

View from Ootacamund, 1869. Photograph by Jim Breeks.

William also wrote to his eldest son:

> My dear Willy,
> Your mother leaves this next week with the children. It will be a sad breaking up
> of the family. I shall feel the absence of all most bitterly. Your mother and baby
> (Kate), I may hope to see again in the autumn, but from your other brothers and
> sisters, as from you my dear boy, it is a long parting…

Lina had taken with her the youngest child, Kate, together with Henry, Lina, James and
Mouse. George and Alfred, the two younger children were left at Guindy. She planned
to return to India in the autumn, bringing Kate back with her, the four other children
presumably being left in England with Lina's mother, Maria Hornby. We can easily
imagine how exciting it must have been for Lina when she arrived back in England to
see Frank, Willy and her parents again and to be in England in April when it is at its
greenest and most beautiful.

It must have felt very odd for both Sir William and Susan to find themselves a family
party of two in the dining room at Guindy, Alfred and George being too young for
grown-up meals. However, the little boys must have been a distraction and cause for
amusement to their father, as very small children can be. Distraction was needed, for
Sir William tells us that "he felt the parting very much."

Susan, now twenty years old, did have to take her mother's place in the home during
these months. Her father, not unnaturally, writes of her much more frequently, "Susan
and I" becoming the standard first person in describing his observations and resolutions,
as she accompanies him on his travels.

There are letters from Susan in existence, written in that summer of 1861 to her
brother, Frank. The first of these illustrates the hazards of travelling, in rather the same
way as William's letter from New South Wales had done. On 15 July 1861, Susan
wrote:

> My dear Frank,
> Papa tells me he has given you an account of our visit to the Godavery, and all
> the scenery, business etc. of our little tour. I have only the little miseries to enlarge
> upon, and among these the insects are the most prominent. Such a place for these
> I never saw. The gentlemen of the party went by day in a steamer, Lady Cotton,
> Rosalie and myself following in a canal boat. We started about dusk, and as soon
> as the sun was fairly down, out came the cockroaches, of all sizes, in swarms.
> When tea came, I climbed up into the roof of our cabin to be out of the way, and
> I would not have a candle for fear of attracting them; but by the starlight I could
> make out myriads of little black things careering in and out of my plate, which as
> you may suppose, damaged my appetite. How we were to sleep was the question
> in my mind, but to my astonishment and relief, about ten o'clock they all disap-
> peared, retiring, I suppose for the night.
>   We sat in the cabin for some time after this and I only saw one of two of patri-
> archal size wandering about as if to see that all their children had gone to bed. I
> had no idea they kept such early hours and treasured up the fact for my comfort

in future, for as Spreadborough says, "I can't abide varmint."

Our experience with insect habits was by no means over. The next day we passed Dowlairsharam. In the daytime, I found only some many-footed, crawling creatures on the walls of my room, and a good many ants on the floor. But, in the morning when I awoke, I heard a regular drip, drip on the floor and imagined the rain was coming in, but when I got up I found that a swarm of large ants had come in through a hole in the wall, through which my punkah rope went, had crawled along the rope for some distance and all dropped on the floor at the same spot, luckily about two feet or so from my head. The floor was quite black with them, in a round spot about two feet across, from which lines radiated in every direction. I got away, however, without being bitten, dressed in a hurry and went off, nearly sick from finding, at the last moment, the decomposed remains of a great crawling animal in the water bottle I had been using.

We were right glad to get onto the 'Dalhousie' again, for this was, compared to our small steamer, a perfect palace.

Your affectionate sister

Susan M.D.

It is interesting and wonderful that Rosalie and Spreadborough were still with the Denisons, although it would have been almost impossible for them to leave for they had become part of the Denison family, since they first came out with them to Van Dieman's Land.

It was during these first few months in Madras that 'Mr B' is mentioned by Susan in her letters to her brother Frank. 'Mr B' was James Wilkinson Breeks, the good-looking young man of 32, who had just been appointed Private Secretary to Sir William on their respective arrivals in Madras – Sir William from Sydney and Jim Breeks from furlough in England. He had been in the Madras Civil Service for the past twelve years, so he knew the country well, spoke the right languages and he was amusing and intelligent. Susan and he saw a lot of each other.

Sir William's "honest conviviality" is well documented and Susan, for all that she accepted the tenets and beliefs of her upbringing, was essentially a person to go her own way. Plain looking, but with bright, sparkling eyes, she was, throughout her life, to read a great deal and to write endless letters. She kept her father's empirical desire to understand how things worked, both in politics and in natural science. Like most of her brothers and sisters, she was amusing, clever and outspoken, found talk irksome and adored music.

Susan probably never knew that her grandmother, Maria Hornby, was illegitimate, simply because she would never have been told. Such information was assumed to be shocking, although Susan was always less shocked by things than the rest of the Denisons and might well have been highly interested by irregularities in her family history.

Susan's great sense of humour, love of colour and character and her intense interest in life around her, vividly displayed in her letters, indicates that she was excited by the nature of Indian life. However, she had little use for the "grand living and the red carpet," which her mother regarded as more or less acceptable, and she chafed over the endless series of dinner parties and levées, with the obligation to maintain suitable conversation with people she would never meet again and always having to take her place in the correct order of precedence. "Dull, formal work," as her father described it. She hunted with the Madras Hunt, of which her father was president, and so did 'Mr B', her father's secretary.

A letter of Susan's, written to her brother Frank, illustrates her almost Dickensian instinct for narrative, in powerful contrast to her father's 'straight' descriptions.

Ootacamund – 15 August 1861:
My dear Frank,
    We stayed at Coimbature that night and the next day and it was arranged that we should get into our transits at ten o'clock that night so as to reach Metapolliam in time to get up the Conoor ghaut (steps leading down to a river for bathing purposes: Hindi) before the sun got hot. There was, however, a large dinner party, then we, that is the ladies, had to change our dresses before starting and were just retiring to do so when we were suddenly summoned to prayers. I am afraid we were not quite disposed for this as we were in a hurry to start. However, there was no help for it and we all knelt down in a rather improper frame of mind to follow, if possible, a lengthy extempore prayer. Dr S, whose unconcealed appreciation of comfort is one of the most amusing things about him, was particularly put out for, being taken by surprise, he unfortunately placed himself in a corner out of reach of the punkah, and between the heat and waiting to get on with our journey, his impatience for the end of the proceedings became irrepressible and vented itself in a sonorous 'Amen', to which he gave utterance at every pause in a prayer by way of a hint that it was time to conclude.

    We got off, however, at last and went on in our transits to a place called Metapolliam where there is a bungalow. Here we put on our riding habits, as well as we could by the light of a tallow candle stuck in a bottle, and went on again for about five miles to the foot of the ghaut where we found our horses waiting. The ride up is charming, though it is steep towards the end and was hot. But, the scenery is beautiful and the delight of feeling a rather fresher breath of air at every turn, and seeing the hot glaring plains further and further below, is something to be appreciated only after some months' experience of the Indian hot season.

    We reached the top of the ghaut at about ten o'clock, nearly a couple of hours later than we ought, and were kindly received by Mr and Mrs Arbuthnot, who occupied a cottage beautifully situated on a hill looking down the ghaut. No descriptions can give you any idea of the scenery, so I shall not attempt it. We remained at Conoor till Saturday afternoon.

    On Friday, we had a very pleasant trip to a point called Lady Canning's Seat, from which there is a beautiful view up, down and across the ghaut. We made our way back by a different path and Dr S had the most dreadful fall I ever saw. He was riding a large, clumsy, ewe-necked horse and as we were going along a narrow path on the side of a steep hill, he stopped to gather a flower. His horse backed just as he reached out his hand for the purpose, its hind legs went over a high bank of stone which supported the road and it fell backwards. Dr S was thrown luckily clear of the animal, but both rolled down the face of the hill for some thirty or forty feet and it seemed to me that the horse rolled over him. I was terribly frightened, thinking he must have been killed. Papa and Uncle Charles (William Denison's brother) were off their horses in a moment, scrambled down to him and found him a good deal shaken and bruised and with a cut on the back of his head. It was a great mercy that the side of the hill was covered in shrub, which broke his fall. It took four people to get him up to the path again, the hill was so steep. Uncle Charles and Papa supported him, one on each side, while two others helped to pull him up. The horse was not injured at all.

William Denison wrote from Ootacamund on 1 September 1861:

> ...We have, as my date will show, fled from the heat of Madras, where the temperature varies from 82° at night to 98° during the heat of the day. The effect of the change of temperature upon the children is very marked. They have picked up both flesh and colour and are twice the boys they were a month ago. It is different, however, with our servants. We are obliged to treat them as exotics, to clothe them warmly and watch over them like hot house plants, and after all, they look miserable and pinched...

A few weeks later, Susan and her father were horror struck at the announcement of the approach of a Rajah. He did not however stay long. Sir William wrote on 23 October 1861:

> He made Susan a present of two peafowls and two wild pigs. To me he gave a young bison, which I have left with the Collector. We had intended to have remained at Windsor... for a couple of days, but my Private Secretary (Jim Breeks) is unwell, having an attack of fever…

The following month, Lina Denison returned to India and life as the Governor's wife continued.

It was said in later years that Sir William was well liked "because he was like an English country squire." He would glean casual remarks about popular feelings and preferences from the barber who cut his hair. But here, as in Australia, William combined a loyalty to his sovereign that was conventional, personal and sincere, with impatience (at times even disgust), at Imperial complacency. He complains in a letter to England, dated 20 January 1862:

> ...Although we heard an account of the death of the Prince Consort, yet the official intelligence which should have come has not reached us, and we have, in fact, no authentic news later than December 10 or 11. I am most anxious to know how the poor Queen has stood the shock.

One wonders whether, on receiving this news, the Denisons wore mourning and, indeed, if this was the correct thing to do two months after the event. He continues:

...yet these people, tenacious of their customs, we believe will change their habits all of a sudden. I am altogether incredulous. We flatter ourselves that we are so pleased with our system of Government that they may prefer that we – aliens in colour, language, customs and religion – should reign over them rather than one of themselves... why should we want to impose our habits and traditions on the Indian? Bosh! How should we like King Mumbo-Jumbo, with a hundred thousand Africans, to set up his throne in London? Certainly, if they are unlike us in many ways, they are like us in this, that they prefer their relations to strangers...

Of whites, very few contemplate this country their home. They look to return to England as the end and sole object of their being.

Sir William further demonstrates his annoyance with the Imperial system in a letter from Ootacamund to Sir Charles Wood, Secretary of State, dated 13 September 1862: [*Worries and Memories of the Indian Mutiny*]

My dear Sir Charles
I have heard from two sources that the natives are beginning to send out chuppatties or cakes as they did before The Mutiny. This would seem to be something analogous to the fiery cross in the highlands. My feeling is that dealing with these people too much according to English principles, we attribute to them feelings which would operate upon us, but which either have no action, or a very different action, upon them. I do not believe, except with perhaps a few exceptions, they care one farthing about the justice as we term it. All they remember – and their memories are very good – is that we have come in as aliens and intruders, having ousted their native rulers, sometimes by the strong hand and sometimes, between you and me, by very dirty processes. We must not expect gratitude or affection from them and must be prepared to deal with them should they be foolish enough to break out a second time, just as their native rulers would do, that is to show but little mercy, to act thoroughly upon their fears.

In October 1862, Lina writes:

I do not think that I shall ever keep pace in my letters with all I have to tell. This Indian travelling is so amusing and letters are so little able to do justice to the scenes. On Monday evening we left Tinnevelly and a palanquin journey through the night brought us to Nagercoil, where we were to rest in a bungalow during the day. The journey was long, very wet and very tiring, but nevertheless, very amusing.

We passed through a native town where people were waiting in crowds to see us. Through the darkness, we had a glimpse of a large elephant with smart red trappings making salaams to us and the people ran by the side of our palanquins with flaming torches till we got a long way past the town. At another place, we crossed the boundary between our territory and that of the Rajah of Travancore and there was some great official or other sent by the Rajah to welcome us to his dominions, but I, unfortunately, had fallen asleep in my palanquin just at this juncture, so missed the ceremony.

I am told that William, who had just fallen asleep, was roused suddenly and, only half awake and conscious of a need for immediate action, but not quite aware of what the occasion might be, stepped hastily out of his palanquin just as he was, without waiting to put on his coat or waistcoat, which he had thrown off for the sake of coolness. So, in the middle of a gazing crowd and all the pomp and circumstance the place could answer, there suddenly emerged the great man in shirt sleeves and with rumpled hair. Not, I am afraid, a very imposing representative of British Majesty!

It was now twenty years since Sir William and Lina had sailed to Van Diemans Land and they were longing to be back in England.

Finally, in 1866, they arrived home and for the first time in fifteen years the Denisons were a united family. For the rest of their lives they lived at a house called Observatory House in East Sheen. It was said that Lina found it difficult to adjust herself to life in England after living so long in government houses, and that she expected everyone to stand up when she entered her box at the opera. However, judging by her letters, I feel that she was far from grand and was very human.

8

Jim Breeks

Jim Breeks's childhood was very different from the Denisons' and Hornbys'. It is necessary to return to 1830 when Jim was born. He was the second son of Richard and Betsy Breeks of Warcop, a village in Westmorland, now part of Cumbria, and one of the most beautiful areas of England.

In 1828, Jim's father ran away with pretty Betsy Wilkinson, the eldest daughter of James Wilkinson, a yeoman farmer, of Low Row, Crosby Ravensworth, only ten miles from Warcop. They were married in Warcop by special licence. They became a famously handsome couple.

Betsy's five brothers, Thomas, William, Robert, Lancelot and James Wilkinson all went out to India, having joined the East India Company. They were all born during the 1790s and the first years of the 19th century. Some of their Dent cousins from Maulds Meaburn were also in India. Of the five brothers, only James did not like India and returned home to farm the family property at Crosby Ravensworth. He never had any teeth and was known in the village as "toothless Jamie." His wife, Frances, was known for her special kind of brandy snaps – how well Jamie managed to eat these crunchy biscuits with no teeth we can only wonder.

There are one or two letters written by Lancelot and Robert to Betsy in which they often ask to be remembered to their friends and relations when she saw them in Appleby on market day. Presents were sent from India, including jewellery in carefully embroidered boxes, earrings, pictures and large, wooden toy animals. The Wilkinson brothers were all in the Bengal and Bombay presidency, except for Thomas, who was in the 6th Bengal Light Cavalry.

In the centre of the village of Warcop was a long, low house, typical of the farmhouses in Westmorland, with a shallow roof, a door in the middle and two windows each side, up and down. Like other houses in Warcop, it was built of red sandstone. At right angles to the house and added on were the stables and the farm buildings consisting of an immense stone barn with a high loft and some outhouses, and at the back a large kitchen, quite separate and only attached to the main house by a narrow passage. This was the home of Richard and Betsy Breeks.

If you stand outside the Breeks' house in Warcop (for the house never seems to have had a name) you can see that this part of the village can hardly have changed at all since the first quarter of the 19th century. However, in those days the village would have been much livelier than it is today because census returns show that there were far more people per house. Families were larger and it wasn't compulsory to send children to school, so they were often to be seen playing in the road or on the village green.

Children would also be seen working in the fields which surround the village.

Some of these fields belonged to Richard Breeks. He, like all the farmers, would have employed children and women as well as men. All through the year women worked in the fields – picking potatoes, cleaning turnips, hoeing and helping in the dairy. During haytime, the whole family turned out to help, as they did when the corn was ready to be scythed. At the end of harvest time the women and children went gleaning in order to help a little with the pittance they earned throughout the year. Some of the poorer people lived in thatched hovels, which are now mercifully extinct. How picturesque the women must have looked in their long dresses with their shawls and bonnets. However, in the winter, not nearly so attractive because they wore anything they could get hold of to keep out the cold. They tucked their dresses into their clogs and wore hessian sacks as aprons.

People living in the village walked and rode and there were always carts of all kinds and wagons and dogcarts, and the occasional carriage and fly and, every now and then, a peddler or a tinker or a knife mender passed. The old people would remember, and sometimes still see, the drovers and their flocks of geese, which were such a menace on the roads, on their way to York, or south to London. It was still common to see packhorse ponies come over the narrow bridge, their panniers filled with wool ready to be spun. It is said today that many a peddler or tinker slept in the hay in the barn belonging to the Breeks's.

There were several inns and far more shops, and more girls were employed in the village also, as servants at Warcop Hall and at Warcop House. They wore print dresses and white stockings and black shoes, which were much prettier than the black afternoon dresses of a later date. The well-to-do farmers, like the Breeks, employed two girls from the village and two men outside. They had one living-in general maid.

Nothing can contrast so well as the England of Burgoyne, and later Knowsley, with the village life of Westmorland. There were two butchers in Warcop and a straw bonnet maker, two grocers, a shoe mender and a blacksmith. There were carthorses, carriage horses and horses to ride waiting at the forge with all its tapping and hammering noises, sounds of shoeing, sparks flying and a pungent, firey smell. There were stonemasons, carriers and two dressmakers.

The Post Office was just opposite the Breeks' house. How exciting it must have been to see the mail arrive and to run across the road to see if there were any letters from India. The length of time which the delivery of letters took at this time is surprising.

Appleby, the county town, was only four miles away from Warcop. Market day was Saturday, just as it is today, and the Breeks family took their produce to sell and took the chance of seeing their Wilkinson relations from Crosby Ravensworth and their Dent cousins from Maulds Meaburn.

The Breeks, who had lived in Burton and Warcop for several generations, owned and farmed their own land. Yeomen were an aristocracy of their own, most of them being able to educate their children at Appleby Grammar School. They were not large landowners, they were not carriage folk and they weren't grand, but they worked extremely hard and they were the 'salt of the earth'. On special occasions, the silver

The Breeks' farmhouse in Warcop.

teapot would be brought out and used and there were lamps instead of candles, and a piano. We know that the Breeks girls all played the piano. Jim, and his elder brother Richard, went to Appleby Grammar School. They would have walked or taken a lift to and from with a local carrier as it would be several decades before Warcop was connected to Appleby by the Eden Valley Railway.

Betsy Breeks's Wilkinson brothers, who were typical Nabobs, had lived in immense comfort in India, having built themselves large bungalows. They were charged with keeping the peace and with the prevention of crime and, as magistrates, they exercised summary jurisdiction and built bridges and roads. They became known in the family as 'the Wilkinson Uncles' and having made large fortunes for themselves in India, retired home to England, establishing themselves in London. Robert lived at 22 Cumberland Terrace, the smart new Nash house in Regents Park. The brothers joined the Oriental Club and as well as properties in London, they bought a house in Westmorland, at Long Marton, only a few miles from Appleby. Like so many of their relations, they always returned to the north.

The uncles had come a long way since they were children in the farmhouse at Crosby Ravensworth. They had lots of money to spend. Uncle William is the uncle we know the most about because when he came back to England, he kept account books of all his expenses and from these we can read of all the things that he did for the Breeks family. His writing was small and neat and the portrait of him in Appleby Moot Hall shows him to have had a round face and a benign expression. William built a home for himself at Warcop – a large white house called Edengate.

When the young Richard and Jim Breeks were aged eleven and twelve, they left Appleby school and went to Blackheath Proprietary School. This schooling was paid for by Uncle William, as were their travelling expenses to London and back home. They stayed the night at the beginning and end of each term with their other uncle, Robert Wilkinson, in his large, comfortable house in Cumberland Terrace. Aunt Noble, a sister of the Wilkinson uncles and Betsy Breeks, also lived at Cumberland Terrace with her brother Robert. As Ellen Wilkinson, she had gone out to India and married a Colonel Noble, but returned to England with him a sick man. He died almost as soon as they reached England and the pretty Ellen, then in her twenties, wore a widow's cap for the rest of her life and was always known as Aunt Noble. She was very small and a dress she wore, of lavender coloured silk from Paris, has been handed down in the family.

We also know, from account books kept by William Wilkinson, that during the 1840s, Jim's mother and sisters stayed at Cumberland Terrace. At Helbeck there are several series of daguerreotypes, the forerunner of the photograph, which were taken by the fashionable M. Claudet of Regent Street. Even if the Breeks lived in a small way, the Wilkinsons saw to it that they paid visits to London. Typical expenses recorded – tips at a toll gates, two shillings for ices, two shillings for Dinneford's Milk of Magnesia and four shillings and sixpence for toothpaste.

We can imagine what kind of holidays Richard and Jim must have had at Warcop. They were taken on 'Trips to the Lakes', which cost £3-10s., they fished in the River Eden and learned to shoot. They must have made expeditions to the nearby Helbeck Woods, which are a paradise for children, with limestone rocks and caves.

When Richard and Jim left Blackheath, they were sent to Haileybury. Jim was the cleverer of the two Breeks boys. The evidence of his scholastic career at Haileybury is shown in the many books which he won as prizes for a wide variety of subjects. Haileybury, or the East India College, qualified young men, who were mostly connected with Directors of the East India Company, for service in India. Subjects such as Orientals, Sanskrit, Persian and Hindustani were taught, as well as Law, both general and Indian. The college buildings were similar in design to those of University College, London, and the little studies were as near identical as possible, each with a small barred window (reminiscent of a prison cell!) and a curtained recess for the bed with a cupboard to one side. Each student was allowed to spend £10 on a carpet, window curtains, a table and four chairs.

The day began at 8am with morning prayers and Bible reading, and ended after a similar observation in the evening. College servants catered for domestic needs. The main part of a student's day was occupied with lectures from 10am until lunchtime, followed by work on his own until 3pm and then taking exercise.

Although discipline was lax, it has been said it was because of Haileybury, that the Indian Empire was administered by men who worked loyally for the 'Company', and though many came from comfortable homes, it seems most of them were found to be instinctive sympathisers with the 'tillers of the soil'. We may be sure that Jim was one of these when, as the son of a small landowner, he passed 1st class into the Presidency of Fort St George, better known as the Madras Civil Service.

Education for the Indian service had, for many people, a drastic finality about it. "India I've been prepared for, India it must be." However, one of the precepts that was most earnestly instilled into the future recruits on leaving Haileybury was that "if we are to govern India at all, we must govern it for the people of India," and therefore that "as the last lesson you will receive on leaving these shores, it is your bounden duty to attempt to govern the people of India by their affection and not by their fears" (*R D Mangles of Haileybury*).

In 1849, Jim's father died at Warcop, at the premature age of fifty. It was not the most auspicious time for Jim to be faced with the immediate prospect of departing the family home for his father had left him as his executor. Betsy, therefore, had staunch and loyal assistance with the legal matters arising from her husband's death, from her brother William Wilkinson, but her feelings, with the entire male complement of her family rapidly disintegrating about her, can all too easily be imagined. However, her five daughters, Elizabeth, Agnes, Mary, Eleanor and Margaret, remained. Liz, the eldest, appears from her daguerreotype to have been a plump, comfortable, motherly looking creature, even at the age of nineteen. Agnes, two years younger, was very good looking and drew remarkably well.

A brief note in the family Bible states that on "8 October 1849, James Wilkinson Breeks left Warcop and, on 20 October, he sailed for India." We may presume that Jim felt considerably troubled at leaving his newly widowed mother, even with the sterling companionship of his eldest sister. In addition, the prospect of ten years in India before he was due to come home again, must have been not a little sobering.

The journey might have taken as long as three months for the Suez Canal did not exist and it meant going round the Cape of Good Hope and then northwards through the Indian Ocean, with the risk of fever and cholera. Jim would have had to furnish his cabin himself and he would have taken furniture, which was saleable on his arrival in Madras, or of use to him in his own bungalow. Some people took their pianos with them, but the sea air was not considered good for the piano. He probably took his own hammer and nails with him too, because so many other people did, to enable him to put up pictures and drawings of his family in his cabin. He would have had an enormous amount of luggage, only a little of which he would keep in his cabin, though he would keep all his books which were a help to while away the time during the voyage. He would have been given an immense list of things which he would need for India and he would have consulted the numerous booklets which were published on what and what not to take. The two important medicines to be taken out were chlordane and quinine.

It is quite likely that Jim knew several other men on the journey, some from Haileybury, and there would also have been men going out to join their regiments and a motley assortment of civilians. He would have had a very good idea of what a journey of three months was like and what life in India was going to be like. It is difficult for us to realise what an enormous number of English people went to India at this time.

The cabins on board were all acutely uncomfortable and passengers always found it difficult to get used to the incessant noise, especially during a gale, and if the ship ran out of coal, which was still fairly common. The sailors sang as they unfurled and furled the sails, and the sails creaked and groaned as they went up and down. It would depend where Jim's cabin was as to whether he heard the sheep and pigs which were taken on board.

For the first part of the journey, Jim would have had farewell letters to write and these would be taken back to England by a homeward bound ship. When this happened, passengers were given a bare ten minutes in which to close up letters to relatives, which were then passed over to the homeward bound ship.

As well as being very cramped and uncomfortable on board, it was incredibly boring, the food got duller and duller and there was nothing to do except read and play cards. It was a welcome relief when they stopped for a few days at Cape Town where the passengers were able to sleep ashore and the ship was replenished with fresh food.

Jim landed at Madras on 3 December 1849. The first approach to Madras was very striking – the low, flat, sandy shore extending for miles to the north and south. "The fort and town are like a vision of excitement," he said. Everywhere was crowded with people of all colours, all wearing gay and bright clothes. There were strange smells of spices and whiffs of curry, and the bright sun shone on the buildings, which had been painted, making them look like marble. Minarets and pagodas were seen rising from the gardens and everywhere were large oriental banyan trees. He would have been surprised that so many of the Indians spoke English.

There was never any attempt to adopt the Indian way of building a house opening inwards onto a courtyard, which would have made it cool and luxurious with verandas, courtyards, fountains and formal gardens. Instead, the classical style was imported bodily and the veranda was not even made wider, but laid bare in order to see the grandeur of Ionic columns. So Jim, on his arrival, would have seen an enormous number of typical English houses built in the grand manner.

On landing at Madras, he would have been immediately greeted by hundreds of Dubashis, with a good command of English, pushing for employment to provide almost any kind of service – to interpret, change money, find servants or tradesmen, go on shopping errands or provide palanquins. Most newly arrived civil servants were able to bring letters of introduction with them from home. Another way of making social contacts was to apply for membership of the Madras Club.

For approximately his first eighteen months in India, Jim was based in Madras itself. After which, in 1851, he was sent to Bellary as an Assistant District Officer. This was a sizeable outpost of the Madras presidency on the river Tungabhadra, three hundred miles to the west. The only building of note there, however, was a fort used by the army. The climate was hot and dry but not unhealthy. Cotton was grown in the fertile areas and leopards roamed the barren, granite hills that overlooked this settlement. During the dry season the river was low and easily fordable, but after the south-west monsoon during the summer, its level rose often by more than twenty feet, its breadth increased to half a mile and crocodiles abounded.

The intense sun was reckoned to be more difficult than anything else for the English to get used to, and there was always the constant risk of fever. In addition, there was a total lack of any form of sanitation in the villages and following the call of nature had become a sort of collective ritual at dawn. Consequently, it is hardly surprising that the land immediately surrounding a village was the most fertile and valuable!

Like his colleagues, Jim Breeks lived in a thatched bungalow, equipped with a punkah with several coolies to operate it in turn. The furniture was such as could be taken to camp when necessary – a collapsible table, a light bed and one or two chairs. (All his servants, bringing china, glass and cooking utensils, would accompany him). The normal diet was curry and rice and whatever meat was to hand, usually fowl of some kind, together with claret. This was usually the same whether at home or in camp, when sticks were collected and a fire started in a hole in the ground. Such was the traditional ingenuity of Indian people in cooking a meal in practically any surroundings.

Serving in this remote area, a civil servant's work tended to combine that of engineer, architect, legislator and diplomat. His day would begin by getting up at six to ride to the scene of, perhaps, some dispute, then he would have a leisurely breakfast and then attend courts. He spent long periods working on his own and very lonely it must have been. News from England was slow to penetrate, but life on the whole was more stable, less disturbed and more patriarchal and personal than in the north where communications were better and the administration more formally organised.

A great deal has been written about the English in India during those pre-mutiny days when Jim Breeks first went out. Young men like Jim were keen and enthusiastic and they all felt that the welfare of the Indian was important, as was teaching them to govern themselves. The Wilkinsons, the old Nabobs of the earlier generation, only went out with the intention of making their fortune and then returning to England to spend it. Haileybury had knocked all that out of the next generation.

To a man in Jim's circumstances, compelled to be jack of a good many trades, a source of frustration at first was the extreme lethargy of the Hindus, so long accustomed to alien presences as to be among the most tolerant people on earth. There were also the complications arising from the caste system with the consequent difficulty of remembering whom it allowed to do what kind of work. For instance, in 1854 there was a bad famine and Jim would have had to organise help, find work for people and make storage places for grain. (During that same year, in England, it was the coldest year for a century. At home, in Warcop, they could hardly have known they had ever had a summer.) Mr Kisch, who was a District Officer at the same time as Jim, wrote home:

> You can have but the slightest idea of the immense difficulty in dealing with a famine in a country like India. You go into a village where most of the natives are Brahmins, the highest caste, and you find among them great distress. Though the men are able to work, the only manual work their caste allows them to touch is agriculture, and this cannot be given to them. When you ask one of these men what work he can do, he answers that he can pray.

In December 1859, after ten years in India, Jim returned to England on furlough for eighteen months. Considerable changes had occurred at home. His uncle, William Wilkinson, had recently died at Edengate in Warcop and left Jim, his only surviving nephew, as his executor. One day his housekeeper fell ill. It is said that his sister Betsy then ran out across the fields from her house, without even putting on her bonnet, and lived at Edengate with her daughters from that day on. It is perhaps more likely that, for practical reasons, Jim's mother and his two unmarried sisters moved in with Uncle William and ran his house for him until he died a few years later.

Elizabeth Farren, later Countess of Derby.

Jane Wilkinson in the old kitchen at Low Row, Crosby Ravensworth.
Oil sketch by Thomas Bland.

Helbeck Hall. Watercolour by Dvid Cox, junior.

. The Madras Hunt, 1865. Jim and Susan Breeks (on her grey Australian 'Launce') and Sir William Denison are eighth, ninth and tenth from the left.

Government House,
Madras.

Daisy Thompson, Jim Breeks' niece..

Jim Breeks' sister Agnes Moore. George Richmond, RA.

Jim Breeks' mother, Betsy ('Granny') Breeks.

Helbeck was only three miles from Warcop and Jim must have known it from his childhood. William Wilkinson on his death left Edengate and the Helbeck Hall estate, which he bought when it came up for sale in 1852, and most of his money, to Jim Breeks. He also left Jim's sisters an annuity of £60 per year. We know from his account books that he had kept three servants, three horses, one phaeton, one gig and three dogs.

Thus Jim can be imagined returning home to be greeted by Dicky, his Uncle William's coachman, and having to accustom himself to suddenly becoming a man of considerable property, as his letters of that date show, being concerned with rents, leases and land improvements. Edengate was larger than the Breeks' house and far more imposing. It had a library, drawing room and study, and eight sizeable bedrooms.

We can imagine also, that it must have taken Jim several weeks to readjust to what must have amounted to a new family. Time blurs our vision, voices and faces alter without our knowing it, for such a destroyer of memories is time. So, on his return, Jim was to find his mother living in greater luxury than she had known during her early married life and three of his sisters were also now married. Agnes was good-looking and became the second wife of George Moore, the flamboyant Cumbrian philanthropist, who was twenty years her senior and very rich. Mary had married the Reverend Henry Chester, and Margaret, having gone out to India a few years previously (possibly to visit Jim), had married an impoverished young engineer, Captain Thomson, and settled there.

Helbeck Hall estate, the setting for a great deal of the Breeks history in years to come, was at that time, rented by one Jeremy Taylor. It was a little smaller than Edengate, but exceptionally well planned so that the exterior appears capacious beyond the scale as judged from inside.

Helbeck was a fascinating place. There are numerous watercolours of the Hall, the wood and Fox Tower which were painted by the Breeks' girls when they had painting lessons from David Cox's son, also called David Cox. Helbeck Wood runs along the steep sides of the Pennine Hills. It is rocky and scrambley, and in various parts of it are great heaps of boulders where lichen and moss and ferns grow. There are said to be caves under one of these gigantic rocks, but they have never been found. The ash woodland is so old that most of the trees are scraggy and bent by the wind. There are seedlings of birch and sycamore, the odd crab apple tree, a few knarled oaks and holly trees. There are ponds and waterfalls and everything is a different height from everything else. In the spring there are masses of primroses and bluebells and some rare exciting plants, and everywhere there are mosses, ferns and patches of bracken.

Higher up is the wood, and above it the jagged, rocky hills, and out of the wood, on a rocky point, is the Fox Tower, which is a folly or view point. It looks like the ruined tower of a castle and is eerie and bleak when the mist is down, though altogether romantic.

Helbeck Hall was built in 1776, with ogee windows – faintly 'strawberry hill' gothic. It is built on the edge of the hill, and on each side there are trees with the wood petering out on the far side of the house. There are a few fine beech trees framing the house, which looks over the valley to the distant Howgills and Wild Boar Fell, all looking today exactly as Uncle William would have seen them in the 1840s.

Jim seems to have spent his leave, not unnaturally, at Edengate. He may have shot on the Helbeck and Warcop fells, with the Prestons and Chamleys, both large families who lived in Warcop Hall and Warcop House respectively, which then both had good grouse moors. We also know from his accounts and letters a good deal of draining, fencing and planting was done at Helbeck during the time he was at home. He had a romantic idea that the Fox Tower would make into a keeper's cottage.

At the end of his leave, Jim left Edengate to return to India. It was on his arrival in Madras that he was appointed Private Secretary to Sir William Denison and met Sir William's daughter, Susan.

Jim is first mentioned in one of Susan's letters to her brother Frank, written from Bishopstown, their country house at Ootacamund in the Neilgherry Hills. It is obvious that she is more than merely impressed by the Private Secretary's prowess and resourcefulness:

Ootacamund, 12 August 1861,
  My dear Frank
  We left Madras on the 26th of last month for the Nilagiris hills.
  We started off, Papa leading, but we had not gone far when a thunderstorm burst upon us. I became very uneasy about my poor parrot, which was in front in a sort of box seat and was getting very wet. The little birds, I got in, cage and all, but Poll's cage was too big to come through the opening. Of course, the stupid creature would not understand what I wanted, or appreciate my motives, and it was only after a long struggle, and getting very wet, that I pulled him out of his cage and got him into the transit, looking very draggled and sulky. My bed too got wet in the struggle.
  I had not finished my battle with the parrot when I felt myself stopping and was told that the thunderstorm had filled a nullah or watercourse, and changed it into a torrent, which they were afraid to cross. Of course, there was a good deal of yelling and noise, in the midst of which I heard Mr B. order my driver to try the stream. We soon stopped, however, turned around and came out again. Papa had, however, got through the place before the water rose, but the rest of us were in our transits and looked disconsolately at each other. It would have been amusing had I not been so uneasy about the result. The torches were flaming and smoking and throwing odd gleams of light on the trees and on the faces of the drivers and the bullocks. I could make out through the clatter that our gentlemen wanted some of the natives to try the depth of the water by wading in, but this they were not at all willing to do. But, after a time, I saw Mr B. himself wading in, followed at some distance by a torchbearer whom he was, in vain, beckoning forward. After a time I heard a splash and Mr B. was, I believe, nearly carried down the stream. This, however, did not disturb him much, for I saw him in a few minutes coolly sauntering back to his own transit, affording a complete illustration of the difference between the Englishman and the native.
  We were now rather in a mess, I thought. We had 50 miles to go and had only done seven or eight. Papa got over the stream and would not know what had become of us. The roads were heavy with rain and four miles an hour is the utmost

Jim Breeks (1830-72)

to be got out of bullocks at the best of times. However, the storm passed over and the stream ran down as fast as it rose, so that in about an hour or so we were able to get across. We found Papa waiting for us at a place called Bowany where the road crosses the Cauvery river and the Bowany by two fine bridges. Both streams were running full and the sight, even by night, was fine.

Papa had been in for more than two hours. He had got his writing case out and was writing away very philosophically, feeling pretty certain that we should turn up. We had some tea at this place and then pushed on, getting to our bungalow about nine o'clock, where we stopped during the heat of the day. We started again at about 2pm and by eight o'clock reached Coimbature, a distance of about 24 miles, where we put up at the house of the Collector.

Little is known of Jim's day to day life working for Sir William Denison, or of his relationship with the family, but it is known that he and Susan became engaged in 1862 at Bishopsdown, the house which the Denisons had taken at Ootacamund. It is not recorded whether the Denisons approved of the engagement, but it is likely they did for both William and Lina had become very fond of Jim as he possessed qualities which William found agreeable. Besides being hard working, conscientious and a good Christian, Jim had a fund of common sense, was amusing, a good sportsman and a very good shot.

Jim's niece, Daisy Thompson, was later to say that it was due to the fact that Jim and Susan saw so much of each other in India that they ultimately fell in love, meaning that Susan was plain and men were not attracted to her. However, Daisy was always the first to praise Susan's qualities of intelligence, humour and integrity, although it surprised her that she had acquired such an attractive and desirable husband as Jim Breeks, who was known for being very handsome.

The marriage took place in February 1863 at Guindy and Susan's mother, Lina wrote the following to Mrs Stanley in England:

> Now let me begin by thanking you for your letter, entering so warmly and affectionately as it does in our interest, and especially into that great one of dear Susan's marriage. Our bride and bridegroom returned to us a few days ago, after a month's stay in the hills, and are here now; but I'm afraid we shall lose them soon, as they expect to start on their homeward journey early next month. We had some trouble and a good deal of cogitation over our list of invitations to the wedding. One element of difficulty was the intense excitement and interest which the upper classes of the native population took in the affair. They had been at us ever since before Christmas in the most point blank way, at one time accosting me with 'Your daughter is going to be married, why not ask me to the wedding?' After some consideration, we decided upon asking some of the leading natives and we asked them, just as we did everyone else, to meet us at the church and to come on here afterwards. We had no formal breakfast but we had the wedding cake and some ices, etc. in a tent on the lawn at the side of the house, and the native guests were most eager to taste the wedding cake and took very kindly to the champagne, which considering that they were Mohametans, I thought rather odd, but I believe they somehow persuade themselves that that sort of effervescing liquor is not wine!

In April 1863, Susan and Jim sailed for England. At this time, agriculture prospered, Lord Palmerston was still Prime Minister and the recently widowed Queen was in retirement at Osborne House. It was a time when crinolines were larger than ever, of frilly *objet d'art* and mahogany filling every house to suffocation, of Charles Dickens drawing large, fashionable crowds to dramatic readings of his works, of decorative cast iron bridges and railway stations.

It was also a time when many thousands of people were dying from the neglect and filth in the workhouses. This was the London Susan was to see for the first time. One wonders what she thought of it all. In later years she describes London as "…so dirty

Susan Breeks with her son Dick.

and the houses all pinched." I imagine that she was thinking of the numerous terraced houses.

What a reunion there would have been with her younger brothers and sisters. Henry, Lina, James and Mouse, who had come to England with Lina two years before and remained there, must have been delighted to see their sister and their glamorous new brother-in-law. Susan stayed at Little Green with her grandmother, old Maria Hornby. What apprehension Susan must have felt on visiting Westmorland to meet Jim's family.

In October 1863, Jim and Susan returned to India and a month later their first son, Richard (Dick) was born at Guindy. It is thought Jim and Susan were living there with Sir William and Lina. It is possible that Richard shared a nursery with Susan's youngest sister, Kate.

9

The Family Firm – Dent and Co.

Jim's cousins, the Dent family from Trainlands, Crosby Ravensworth, ten miles from Warcop, were running the family firm of Dent and Company in the Far East. The firm owned clippers, which were the fastest boats in the world. They had to be fast because they shipped tea from China, which would lose its flavour in the hold, and therefore the first boat back to London was thought to have, and usually did have, the best tea. These ships, together with their great speed, were also usually fully armed.

At this time, despite its many wars, China was full of precious and infinitely beautiful objects of all kinds, which had been in great demand in this country for many years. So, as well as tea, the clippers had brought silks, jade, porcelain and furniture to supply a ready market in eighteenth century England. Tea was the principal merchandise wanted for London and the whole set up of trading in the Far East had an enormous appeal to the Dents, even if at times they wanted to be at home in Westmorland.

The opium trade in the Far East was also lucrative. Lancelot Dent was out in Canton, China, and the firm of Dent and Co., together with the better known Jardine & Matheson, had for some years been trading (or to put it bluntly, smuggling) opium, from Calcutta to China. Lancelot, was reputedly a soft-hearted man, but he had a personal dislike of Mr Jardine and they were in deadly competition. The opium trade, however, for the time being, boomed.

Up until 1834, the East India Company had had the sole right in Britain of trading to China and in the early eighteenth century the company had firmly established itself as the chief European agency for trading with the country. For centuries, opium poppies had been cultivated in Bengal and the East India Company encouraged the people of Bengal to continue growing the poppies, which were then sold in Calcutta. The proceeds of these sales went, of course, into the pockets of the Company's servants. The opium was packed into chests and stowed in the holds of the tea clippers, each clipper taking 100-200 chests and the chests were eventually sold in the Hongs of Canton. It is reputed that Jardine & Matheson sold each chest for around £20. The Chinese people had, of course, smoked opium for years and the best opium came from Bengal.

Then, in 1834, the Chinese government banned the importing of opium because of the detrimental effects it was having on the people, and the East India Company opted out of shipping it to China. Dent and Co., and Jardine & Matheson, however, carried on the trade and they virtually held the monopoly. These firms would use their ships to take the opium to China, but would anchor off shore and transfer the cargo onto 'receiving ships' which would transport the opium ashore where it would be sold in the opium dens.

In 1851, much to everyone's surprise, Lancelot's brother, Wilkinson Dent, arrived out in Hong Kong. In later years, he would be known by his nephews and nieces as "old Wilky Dent." By 1859, he was one of the 'old residents' of Canton, known to be a kind and good hearted man, though generally feared in the office. Wilky Dent was the second largest importer of opium and was referred to in some quarters as "that arch smuggler Dent."

Lancelot came home to Westmorland and built a new, vast and extraordinary house quite near to Trainlands. The front door of 'Flass' is at first floor level and inside the house, hundreds of steps go down to the floor ahead where the drawing room and other principal rooms are situated, looking out over the River Lyvennet. A beguiling and, somehow, unreal house, Lancelot filled it with the lavish furniture and objects he brought back from China – a Mandarin's bed, Chinese furniture, wallpaper, and porcelain. At the centre of the house is a perpetually cold, inner hall, with a balustrade round it at a great height. Perhaps Lancelot had forgotten the cold in Westmorland, after so long being used to the heat in the Far East.

In 1856, Old Wilky Dent was still out in Hong Kong, but said to be "too busy." Tom Leslie later accused the Dents of being dictatorial with their colleagues: "It is perfectly absurd the way Wilkinson Dent goes on professing great things and doing nothing."

Captain Lindsey Anderson gives us an account of *A Cruise in an Opium Clipper* – his voyage in *The Eamont*, a clipper belonging to the Dents and named after a river near Trainlands. He tells how it skirted the coast of China trying to find 'receiving ships' so that the clipper could unload its opium and speed away. The clippers were armed, fast and adventurous.

In the early 1860s, it was rumoured that Dent, Palmer and Co. (as the firm was now called) had not been well managed for some years and according to Basil Lubbock in *The Opium Clippers*, John Dent, Thomas's brother, had been reckless and 'too adventurous' with his side of the business. He was possibly tactlessly allowing his clippers to unload straight onto the Old Hongs on the Yangtze, tempted by the ease with which the opium disappeared into the dens, rather than taking a little more time to find the 'receiving ships'. Also at this time, there was the rise in the trade in Indian tea and the advent of steamships. The Thames Shipbuilding Co. launched a racing steamer, the *Ly-ee Moon*, for Dent, Palmer and Co. and a fleet of racing steamers especially designed for carrying opium from India to China. Thomas Dent called Dent, Palmer and Co., "As sure as the Bank of England."

In the mid-1860s, however, things were not so easy for the Dents. Business was poor and its failure to survive the black year of 1865 has generally been ascribed to the rashness of John Dent. Both the Breeks and Wilkinson families had been anxious for Jim to join the firm and because he had had attacks of fever, which was so prevalent in the plains near Madras, it was clearly sensible to be out of India, though he hadn't served his full time.

So, Jim and Susan and their baby, with Rosalie, the Denison's nanny, who had looked after Susan in the past, travelled to England. Their luggage was formidable and included a great many books, early photographs and pictures of friends and relations, as well as guns and fishing rods. They settled into Gloucester Place, near Hyde Park.

It was the usual terraced house, recently built, on several floors, with a kitchen in the basement, servants' rooms in the attic, and a floor for the nursery above the bedrooms and living rooms. Uncle Robert Wilkinson and Ellen Noble were still not far away in a rather grander house in Cumberland Terrace, and Uncle Thomas Wilkinson in Hanover Square, also a large palatial house.

For Susan, who had never been to England, let alone London, it must have been an exciting time, though I can't help feeling that she would have preferred Westmorland and its beautiful countryside.

Mrs Breeks and Liz were living at Edengate, William Wilkinson's large house in Warcop. There were so many relations for Susan to meet and so much to take in. Jim wrote letters to agents with his plans for Helbeck. Trees were to be planted and landscape architects were written to. A new road was to be built for the Hall and there were other business affairs that Jim would need to see to. They were supremely happy. Then a ghastly cloud loomed – was Dent and Co. safe?

Jim was advised by Thomas Dent, who was now head of the firm in England, that he should wait before putting his money in. Thomas seems to have been unable to control John's activities from England and he was also querying some of the bills and accounts. He may have seen trouble ahead and warned Jim, but it is doubtful he would tell Jim the whole truth. It must have been during a short spell when things quietened down that Jim eventually joined and put £60,000 or £70,000 into the firm.

On 9 July 1867, the firm of Dent, Palmer and Co. declared itself bankrupt. The fleet had been sold a few months prior to this for roughly £183,000. Writing to his father in England, young Alfred Dent declared, "It was a bitter moment when the house flag was brought down. I am glad however that they are to remain under the English flag and the captains and crews to be kept on as before. Dent and Company's shippers were the only ones who knew the Yangtze and their steamers were never ashore."

John Dent sailed home to face his London partners – Thomas, the senior partner and original founder of the China house, and his brother Wilkinson Dent. Meanwhile, young Alfred, Thomas's son, had worked like a Trojan to "save the face of the family" and he did this to such good effect that by 1868 Alfred Dent & Co. was doing business in Shanghai in the old hong.

In retrospect one can't help wondering if Jim was altogether wise in ever considering joining the firm. The advantage was that he would be in the office in London rather than in India, which would be good for his health, and he couldn't afford to live if he was without a job. But one wonders how he would have fared in the expanding world of commerce, let alone the opium trade, after administering justice for so long out in India.

As it was, Jim had no option but to return to work in India, in spite of his weak health. It is a comfort to know that in future years Alfred Dent and his sisters would go to Helbeck to visit Susan, Jim's widow, and the Dents and Breeks were always friendly towards one another.

10

Ootacamund

In November 1867, Jim and Susan sailed for India for the last time. On this occasion, he was to be the Commissioner at Ootacamund, in the hill country. What knowledge we have about their time in India is gained from the contents of the many letters Jim wrote during the months after his return. He wrote from Ootacamund on July 30 1868:

> We are most fortunate to have secured the Hill appointment. It is everything for me and I am working hard to satisfy Lord Napier's [Governor of Madras] selection as far as possible. I have a good deal to do in the Revenue line and two Court days a week so my hands are full…

The following month he wrote to a friend:

> My dear Sanderson
> Here I am, Commissioner of the Nilagiris Hills and am hard at work from 11 to 6 daily. I am, as you may imagine extremely thankful for the appointment and I trust by hard work to give some sort of satisfaction. At present everyone is grumbling and everything is in arrears, but bye and bye with patience and perseverance I trust to get matters straight...

In the same month he writes complaining of the lack of a good map:

> A district officer without a map is like a ship without a compass; could you kindly give me a helping hand in the matter and procure for me the best maps of the Hills on the largest scale procurable… Rain, rain is the order of the day – the monsoon promising to be a good one.

One of Jim's maps, in a well worn case, still exists.

There were also practicalities to see to, as the following letter shows, but there is need to consider his financial constraints too:

> Dear Sir,
> I want you to help me get a good riding horse for my wife for the Hills. I can't afford more than 600rs. I should like the nag to be a powerful one so that he might carry me on occasions. If in your travels you meet with a likely looking animal, you would make all due enquiries about it and send me up sharp. I don't want a thoroughbred for this place, but a nice handy hack such as a lady would not be

ashamed of riding, but one that would stand hardish riding which you remember my wife is partial to.

Some of Jim's letters at this time show that he was still very much feeling the devastating effect of the demise of Dent & Co. On 3rd October 1868 he was writing from Ootacamund to his cousin, John Dodd, a relative, who had also lost money in the family firm:

My dear John,

Lo! My Commission.

Well, you see Dent & Co. has done for me as I fear it has for you. It has cost me up to this close upon £30,000 – however, £10,000 which our good Uncle Robert took off my hands. Fortunately I had not resigned the Indian Service otherwise there literally would have been nothing for us but the poorhouse. When I shall ever get home again I cannot venture to think. Probably never.

I hope you, however, are pushing away – you are several years younger and have time to reprieve. I have nothing to look forward to but my pension of £800 a year.

I am particularly lucky in getting this District – 7,000 feet high – we live in a climate and enjoy a wood fire every night and no mosquitoes. If I can do anything here – write – and it will give me pleasure to be of use.

My wife presented me with a little girl the other day. We now have a boy and a girl and I hope we may stop at that figure for rice is dear.

You hear, I dare say, very regularly from home. I left them all last November as much as usual – the elders looking as they did when I first went to India.

My wife desires her remembrances, and with same from self.

The little girl Jim refers to is Lena, a sister to their son, Richard, who had been left in England with Jim's sister Liz, who was living at Edengate.

In another letter from Ootacamund, dated 30th October 1868, Jim writes:

My dear [illegible name]

My plunge into business was a failure and cost me £30,000. Dent and Co. failed and ruined me. Fortunately I had not resigned my commission service and here I am back again without a farthing and beginning life again.

Such are the ups and downs of three years at home, in a state of panic, which has thickened my skin, but otherwise I am sound and shall die game I hope.

I have got charge of this Hill District and here I hope to remain for years until I am kicked out of the Service as a stupid old fool…

Jim and Susan lived at Bishopsdown, the house where they had agreed to become man and wife, but the house was in a poor state and in February 1869, Jim was writing to Mr Arbuthnot, the accountant, regarding some essentials for the house:

The next point I want to ask you about is whether if the Govt. grant the 500 I can recommend by way of compensation – you can permit us to lay it out in furniture for the house sending you vouchers for everything we purchase. I ask this because I think it ought to be spent this way and because my wife and I having to live in the house are likely to be the best judge of what is wanted I may briefly mention some things that we can hardly do without:

> Drawing room carpet
> Drawing room lamps
> Dining room lamps
> Dining room carpets.
> Tubs, garden implements – no fork and only one spade.

You yourself know the state of a good deal of the furniture so I need go no more into particulars – the commodes are all broken etc. …there are a quantity of broken chairs, beds and suchlike – I think it would be far better both for us and the owner, if we were allowed to send all such articles to auction to sell for whatever they might fetch and remit the proceeds to you. It would clear the place of much rubbish and enable me to have but one list of serviceable articles for which we would be responsible.

An order sent by Jim to Messrs. Daniell & Co. of Bond Street London, requests:

Sirs,
Would you be good enough to send us via Cape as soon as possible.

12 tumblers	12 finer glasses
18 claret glasses	12 coolers
12 champagne	6 teacups
12 liqueur	6 coffee cups
6 soup plates	6 pudding plates
18 wine glasses	1 claret jug

They must all be of the same pattern as those you supplied me with in 1865 and subsequently in 1867 as per Bill E508 enclosed for reference.

On 13th August, an order was sent from Ootacamund for provisions:

> 1 dozen quarts vinegar
> ½ a dozen pots anchovy paste
> ½ a dozen bottles of olives
> ½ a dozen pots crystallised fruits
> ½ a dozen pounds arrowroot
> ½ a dozen pounds sago
> ½ a dozen pounds tapioca
> 3 bottles almonds and raisins
> 4 one pound tins redcurrant jelly
> 4 two pound tins gooseberry jam
> 3 bottles apples

4 pounds macaroni
4 hundred weight primrose soap
3 dozen tins cornflour
3 tins Huntley and Palmers arrowroot biscuits
6 tins Oxford saugages
6 Dutch cheeses
12 pound tins salmon
9 pound tins oysters
9 pound tins lobsters
9 pound tins mackerel
9 packets of plate powder
12 bottles mustard
12 bottles salad oil
2 loaves sugar.

The jams should be sent in tins, the last were in jars and leaked. One or two of the tins of salmon and oysters were not quite full.

As well as making the house comfortable, Jim and Susan worked hard on the gardens, ordering many seeds and plants to be sent from England. Jim worked very hard to justify being given his post in Ootacmund. He was responsible for the management of the whole area, on behalf of the Government, and overseeing the administration of justice. He was also involved in several projects in his district, many concerned with improving living conditions for the native people. In October 1870, he organised an exhibition which included exhibits of pottery, crafts, etc. from the various tribes of the Nilagiris, together with exhibits of coffee, Cinchona and plants.

The exhibition was a great success. Lord Napier, who had succeeded Sir William as Governor of Madras, came to open it. After the event, in a letter dated 5 December, Jim wrote to his Uncle, Robert Wilkinson:

The exhibition went off very well – Lord Napier expressed himself surprised and pleased. We had a public dinner for him of which I had to be chairman and propose his health after the Queen – he replied and spoke for half an hour or more and belaboured me with praises too much – I fancy he is a polished humbug!

Jim and Susan's eldest child, Richard, now called Dick, remained in England and was being brought up by Liz at Edengate. He would naturally have been sent to stay with his other grandparents, Sir William and Lina Denison, at times and was mentioned regularly in correspondence. Jim talks of him in a letter to Sir William, dated March 1868, when arrangements were being made for Dick to join his parents in Ootacamund.

My dear Sir William

We are greatly pleased with Mamma's account of Dick. I wish you could see Lena – she is so nice and fat and laughs all day long. We are still perplexed about having Dick out, even at the end of this year. His stomach and his liver are his

weak points and we are occasionally hearing of children of his age here who have
to be sent away. The sun is amazingly hot in the middle of the day and the nights
are very cold with ice and frosts. We have not had a drop of rain for two or
three months and this is likely to go on till April or May. To grown up people
who when they go out take an umbrella and so forth, it's charming weather,
but somehow it's somewhat trying to children of Dick's age who cannot be
kept in and whose constitution seems to be more easily affected by such violent changes of temperature.

So, Dick did not go out.
   On 7th March 1869, Jim wrote from Ootacamund:

I am making a collection of the Nilagiris woods in pieces eighteen inches long
and about three or four in diameter. I want to cut each piece and polish the face.
Can you tell me how this is best done, what tools I should use and what polish?
I propose doing the cutting and polishing myself in the Monsoon evenings while
Susan reads aloud. In her readings she always manages to keep herself awake by
sewing or something while I, who am most abominably sleepy, have now nothing
in which to employ my hands and am driven to walking about and all sorts of uncomfortable positions to stave off the enemy.
   We are staying away from Church today as Susan did not feel like going. I was
going out tomorrow with my tents again but as Susan cannot come with me I will
put off going till Tuesday or Wednesday.

Shortly after their arrival in India, a decision was made to file a lawsuit against Dent &
Co. in order to try and retrieve some of Jim's capital. Jim though seems to have some
reservations. He wrote to William Denison from Oootacamund:

…I am rejoiced to hear that you are keeping an eye on Uncle Robert – once he
has broken ice and burnt his boats he is the <u>rashest</u> man alive and could be led
into anything.
   …Uncle Robert has consented to the Bill being filed [ie the claim against the
Dents being commenced] and that so far all is well but it's the next step that I am
apprehensive for if they do not show signs of agreeing to some compromise in
some way or other is it worth while proceeding with the case?
   George Moore [husband of Jim's sister Agnes] knows my Uncle thoroughly and
he will tell you how simple he is and how easily anybody with a little primness
and tack can extract anything out of him.

He also wrote to his Uncle:

It's the next step that we have to take that makes me anxious – I see so much of
law expenses here that I am loath to advance further when our strength merely
lies in their weakness. It is for us to establish our claim and unless our case will
stand throughout by itself on its own legs, however weak their case may be and

Jim Breeks with his daughter Lena in about 1870.

however humiliating and discreditable their defence, the judgement will go against
us and we shall have costs to pay.

Another letter from Jim, dated 21 February, to his Uncle Robert refers again to the lawsuit and appears to demonstrate some of Jim's anger and disappointment at his treat-
ment:

> My dear Uncle,
>   By this mail via Southampton I have sent you my watch and would be greatly
> obliged to you if you would quickly take it to Frodsham's and direct them to repair
> it or clean it or do whatever is necessary and send it out to me again as soon as
> they can. Without my watch I suffer great inconvenience as in the course of busi-
> ness I have a number of engagements and am now always at a loss for the hour...
>   I am sorry to think that J. Dodd somewhat reckless in his private expenses à la
> China – I confess that when a man is 28, if I still find him extravagant in his private
> life, (that is) living beyond his means, I could put little trust in him in his public
> or any other capacity.
>   ...I approve of your permission of Mr Rooper to file a bill: the shot is worth 60
> or 70 pounds. I am apprehensive that it will not lead to any great results; however
> it will enable Mr Rooper to see their answer and speak with Freshfields (solicitors)
> which will give him a clearer view of the whole case as it stands between us. He
> has not written to me as suggested. Probably he has not time, and as you and Sir
> William are looking into the matter he may think there is no necessity to write.
>   The indisposition to yield on the part of Dent, Palmer and Co. will (I expect)
> arise from the other partners between Dent and us. I am quite certain that Mr
> Dent is just as convinced as I am that he <u>withheld</u> from you and me at the time
> what he knew he was bounded to tell us and which if he had told us would have
> ended in Dent & Co. being set apart to run at the risk of the old partnership. Nay
> more, he made use of words about the safety of my capital, twice in answer to
> questions from me, which he must have known and felt were not justified by the
> state of the accounts, or why take up the position he did within a few weeks of
> my joining and threaten to stop all business with Dent & Co. if the account was
> not squared – it is utterly impossible to reconcile this attitude of theirs with RD's
> assurance that my capital was 'safe as if it were in the Bank of England'.
>   Nevertheless the other partners were not direct parties to all this and Mr Dent's
> account to them of what took place may differ very far from actual fact and thus
> as it falls in with their interest to believe what he says to them they will resist and
> say we have no case.

In a later letter to Sir William Denison, Jim wrote:

> I understand Mr Rooper has rec'd Dent and Palmer's answer to my Bill and ac-
> cording to Uncle Robert he thinks their case stronger in a legal point of view than
> he contemplated. I was afraid of this. Indeed, Norton (here) prepared me for this
> – I suppose I shall see their answer in due course through Mr Rooper. In the mean-
> time I enclose you Uncle Robert's last letter from which you will see that such
> matters so unnerve him that he is really worth nothing – and if he is called to court

he can remember nothing and would really do more harm than good – it has been my feeling of insecurity upon all matters in which he has taken part that has led me all along to think that I should make nothing out of the Bill.

The case drifted on, with further correspondence between Jim, William Denison and his Uncle Robert. However, rather than reimbursing Jim, the lawsuit was actually costing him money and he wanted to withdraw. He wrote to his uncle on 5 December 1869:

I have two or three letters of yours to reply to – and now that our exhibition is over I hope to be more regular in my correspondence.

I have not yet seen D & Co.'s answer – the paper must have gone down in the Casualic as I suspected and informed Mr Rooper. However I have written strongly to Sir W D and I hope he will at once induce Mr Rooper to withdraw the Bill with the best grace and as little expense as possible.

The moment I have seen the answer and Bristowe's opinion, I will write most plainly to Mr Rooper and order him to withdraw and stop as best he can. I do not like to take this decided step until I have seen their answer and B's opinion.

I have your letter of 4 November informing of the result of the arbitration with …Dent who has to pay £4,500 arbitration fees. I suppose this sum will help to swell the account on the credit side of DP and Co. I confess I do not thoroughly understand their accounts even yet. I must try and give a night to them and see how these dividends and Wilky Dent's payments leave me.

In another long letter to Sir William Denison, dated 12th December 1869, he wrote:

…The fact is that although I have not yet seen DP and Co's answer to my Bill, nor Mr Bristowe's second opinion, I am persuaded that we shall act wisely in withdrawing and saving further expense. If we cannot withdraw each party paying his own costs, still I say withdraw and pay D… costs.

…I should like much to know what my costs have been up to this if you can get such a mystery out of Mr Rooper. The curse of law in England, indeed, everywhere, is that you cannot forecast your expenses – arithmetic is of no use.

I shall be anxious to hear the result of your conference with Uncle Robert and Mr Rooper. Both Susan and I are in favour of stopping all further proceedings and we trust that you have come to the conclusion to order Mr Rooper to withdraw the suit at once on the best terms he can make for us.

My last letter from Elizabeth makes us more anxious than ever that this should be done as we learn from her that old Mr Dent is dying and I had rather pay and lose than distress his last days.

This news of Thomas Dent's ill health persuaded Jim to end the lawsuit. He and Susan felt they could not continue to cause any further anxiety or worry over the affair and, therefore, Jim gave instruction to withdraw. He wrote to his Uncle Robert on 2 January 1870:

The Ootacamund Exhibition, 1869. Photograph by Jim Breeks.

I must begin by wishing you and all with you a Happy New Year and may God bless you all and preserve you in health and strength.

Since last writing to you I have heard of Mr Dent's state of health and this decided me at once to write to Sir William to direct Mr Rooper to withdraw the suit on whatever terms he could get – if I have to pay their costs I must pay. I would rather do so than let the suit worry him in his last illness – with the other partners of the firm I have nothing to contend so to speak for they know nothing of the exact words that passed between Mr Dent and us, on which our whole case rests. It is curious that I have never yet seen D P & Co.'s reply to Mr Bristowe's second opinion although I wrote long ago to Mr Rooper to draw his attention to the probability of the papers having gone down in the Carnatic. I have got no answer to the letter from Mr Rooper and no papers have yet arrived.

When the suit is withdrawn (and the sooner the better) I shall be much obliged to you if you will ask Mr Rooper to make out a bill of all costs from beginning to end and let me have the same and I will remit him the amount.

I enclose you an open letter to Mr Dent which after showing to Sir William and Mr Rooper if you all approve I should like you to give to Mr Dent by way of coming to a reconciliation with him.

It was a relief that things were finally being concluded and Jim and Susan wanted to repair any ill feeling that may have been caused. This was the purpose of Jim's open letter to be approved and passed to Thomas Dent.

Earlier in 1869, the health of Jim's mother had been deteriorating. In a letter from Ootacamund, dated 1st May, Jim wrote:

My dear Sir William

Our letters make us anxious about my dear mother, but we live in hope that the change to the north where she will get among her old haunts and find more bracing air will revive her. I cannot however get rid of the fear that this giddiness and failure of health at her age will prove the beginning of the end... Year by year only adds to the lamentable signs, which meet you everywhere, and in every shape, of the ruin of the Indian Army...

In June 1870, Liz wrote from England to tell Jim and Susan that Granny Breeks had died at the home of their sister Mary Chester at Easington.

Edengate, May 31st 1870
My dearest Susan and Jim,

I hardly know how to tell you the <u>awful</u> news that our darling mother has been taken from us. In my last letter I told you that she was ailing but both she and <u>we</u> made light of it and thought it was only one of her old attacks. She was no better next day so we had to give up coming home of course and I telegraphed to John our change of plans, but <u>still</u> we were not alarmed, nor was the doctor. He came four times on Friday and thought her better in the evening at eleven o'-clock when he left. On Saturday morning at nine o'clock he came again. The moment he saw her on Saturday he was alarmed and at once told us she was in danger and we must send for any friends who wished to see her! Even then I could not believe it – for I had seen her as I thought so much worse so often in the Spring!

So we telegraphed to Dr Charleton of Newcastle and to Agnes and Eleanor. Mary and I never left our darling's bedside after that. Henry Chester came up at once and told her we had sent for another doctor and then he stayed with her. We all knelt down together and said the Collects in the Prayer for Visiting the Sick. She seemed quite to understand her end was near. She must have seen it in our faces. When the doctor came again, which he did at 9 o'clock, he told her not to get up again and she smiled so beautifully at him and said, "Very well, I won't for I am very tired." She said to me afterwards she wished she was at home. The doctor was in incessantly and said he never saw <u>anyone</u> sink so fast, and a little before two o'clock in the afternoon she passed away so peacefully and beautifully with her eyes closed as if she were asleep! I never saw her look so beautiful as she did afterwards with such a lovely smile on her face!

Dear darling, I can't believe she has gone and I am so heartbroken to think how dear Jim will feel it – what a sorrow and grief it will be to you both, to think you will never see her bright face again! The home can never be what it has been without her. She was placed in a leaden coffin on Saturday night and at seven o'clock on Sunday morning, Agnes arrived. It was a sad, heartbreaking day and quite everybody in Shields was so kind we were quite overpowered.

June 1st – the letter from Liz at Eden Gate, Warcop, continues:

Must try and finish my letter today. On Monday, Agnes and the children (Dick, Birdie and Daisy) and I came home. What a coming home it was! The house looked so fresh and the Library quite beautiful, but <u>she</u> has never seen it! We have arranged to have a village funeral so she will be followed by all her old friends whom she loved so much. I cannot tell you how grieved and shocked all the village are. The coffin arrived this morning containing all that is left of her on earth and this afternoon the Chester trio are come, and this evening, George (Moore), Uncle Robert and Eleanor arrive. Agnes has also sent for Newbold and Potter (family retainers). The funeral is tomorrow.

We have received such kind letters from everybody – but the kindest and nicest of all is from Lady Denison! She does feel so much for you both – but feels that you are so completely all in all to each other that you will help each other to bear the sorrow and we, my dearest Susan, do rejoice that you are Jim's wife and that he has you with him to help him in his bitter grief! Dick has shown his sorrow by being more than usually affectionate and clings to me more than ever, but they all have felt it, dear little things, especially when they say their prayers! She does not need our prayers now! <u>Thursday</u> We have just returned from Church and our darling mother rests in her last resting place. It is a lovely day! Uncle Robert, Eleanor and George Moore arrived last night and the Chesters yesterday afternoon. Poor Uncle R looked very ill and nervous!

God bless you both and comfort you.

<u>Everybody</u> in the village has attended the funeral! It has been done exactly as

my dear father's was done and I am sure just what she would have liked. Newbold and Potter are here and have helped bear her body to its last home.

Ever and ever my dear brother and sister.   E Breeks

Although Liz's descriptions may sound too intimate and strange to our ears, it does give a broad picture of the outlook and affection of the Breeks' family, as well as illustrating their sentiment, and this was, of course, typical of the time in which they lived. This letter (now almost yellow in colour) with it's thick, black edging, must have been read several times over by Jim and Susan before it was finally put away.

Later this same year another son was born to them, whom they called Charles, and on 11th January of the next year, 1871, Susan wrote to Liz from Ootacamund:

Dearest Liz,

No letters this week. The mail is expected, I believe tomorrow, Friday. I wrote last on Thursday. We have had a quiet week except for a very troublesome incursion of our two Mr Savages who came to luncheon on Saturday, a thing which I always hate. They are two big, rather stupid looking men, one especially dense and irritating. He managed to tread on my corn twice during dinner – once by asserting in the way of English travellers in India, who will know more about it than residents, that the climate is healthy (I asked why Life Insurance Policies charged double rates – but he still did not seem to hear the force of the argument).

On Tuesday we took advantage of Jim's holiday to go and open some cairns about five miles off. We spent the whole day there, I occupying myself by sketching one of the Toda (tribe of the Nilagiris Hills) conical temples which stands in a most picturesque place on the top of a ridge in a gap in the middle of a pretty little wood and looks down to the low country. Jim occupied himself with the cairns at the top of the neighbouring hill, but they had been rifled and nothing was found but some fragments of pottery as well as a spear. This afternoon Jim is going with Mr Metz to open some more and will be away till Sunday morning. Meanwhile I am expecting the Jansens back again and a horrid nuisance – I hope they won't stay long. I am glad to say that they are going to carry off the stag which was presented to us the other day, greatly to my disgust as they are the most dangerous things in captivity.

We are still in trouble with Charles who is quite the naughtiest boy of his age I know and will not go to sleep except in Leotine's arms. I am insisting on Leotine fighting the point, but as Lena says, "he cries dreadful" and frightens me with the idea he will make himself ill. I must finish as I have several things to do.

In November of that year, Jim and Susan's last child, William was born, and also during this year, Sir William Denison died at East Sheen. We can be sure that all the Denisons felt his death very much, particularly Susan who was always devoted to her father. Sir William had been active since his return to England and in 1869 he was writing his memoirs. He was also Chairman of a Royal Commission which was to enquire into the prevention of pollution of rivers. Shortly before his death, he wrote a pamphlet called *Advice to Children* in which he earnestly recommended that his children "should

The Breeks Memorial School, Ootacamund, 1873.

combat that tendency to argument which I am afraid you have, to a certain extent, inherited from me."

The following year, in the spring of 1872, Jim was spending all his spare time collecting examples of the work of the Hill Tribes for the Calcutta Museum. In June 1871,
the Trustees of the Indian Museum in Calcutta, had written to Lord Napier, Governor
of Madras, and others, regarding "the importance of devoting a section of the Indian
Museum to illustrations of the state of the arts among the aboriginal and other jungle
races in India and its Dependencies."

A month later, in a letter dated 3 July 1871, Jim replied to Lord Napier, gladly ac-
cepting the commission to "procure a collection of arms, ornaments, dresses, manu-
factures, etc. that will serve to illustrate the habits and modes of life of the jungle tribes
of Nilagiris…" He obviously feels the work is very worthwhile and somewhat overdue.
His letter states, "I am glad the matter is receiving attention, late in the day as it is, for
year by year the Nilagiri tribes at any rate are abandoning their distinctive customs."

Jim had intended to finish this work by the autumn of 1872 for presentation to the
Madras Government. Most of the information had been obtained and a rough draft
written by early summer of that year. As well as writing the book, Jim had also taken
on the Commissionership of more land which was in a particularly fever-ridden part of
the hills.

Before the work could be finally completed, in June 1872, he caught a fever and
died within a few days.

When news of Jim's death reached England, George Moore wrote in his diary:

> It is difficult to believe that Jim Breeks is dead. I never loved any man more. He more than came up to anything I had heard of him and I heard of him from my wife from morning to night. My faith is strong but it is impossible to understand why he of all men should be taken.
>
> He was the life and soul of everything in Ootacamund. There was some feeling when his name was mentioned as the first Commissioner, that the welfare of the place was to be sacrificed to the necessity for providing for one who could not reside on the Plains on account of weak health. A few days served to dispel this notion. Before Mr Breeks and his admirable wife had been there a few days, everyone knew that the right man was in the right job. Indefatigable, a cheerful and considerate Chairman, never a hasty word, his judgement remarkably sound. His character had no grain of affectation. There was nothing so touching as his funeral. As the procession wound down from Bishopsdown, it was met at every turn by mourners comprising every class of community. We may be sure he was no ordinary man.

In the church, black crepe was draped over the seat where Jim usually sat. The Breeks' Memorial School in Ootacamund still exists. The graveyard is full of large, ivy-covered tombstones and somehow and in some ways, the name of Jim Breeks remained.

11

Susan's Letters

After Jim Breeks's death in 1872, Susan brought her three younger children, Lena, Charles and William, back to England, and settled down to live in Westmorland. She also undertook the task of completing the book her husband had been working on before his death, about the tribes of the Nilgiris. A huge amount of material had been collected, together with numerous photographs, with which Jim had not been totally satisfied, the allowance of 1,000 Rupees not being enough to cover the engagement of a professional photographer. However, Susan was determined to complete the work and this resulted in the publication of *An Account of the Primitive Tribes and Monuments of the Nilgiris* by the late Jim Breeks. These provide a fascinating record of the five tribes Jim studied. The book was published in 1873 and includes photographs and illustrations.

Susan, joined Liz at Warcop, who had been looking after Dick and Birdie and Daisy Thompson. She spent part of the next ten years at Edengate and part in East Sheen with her mother, Lina, now a widow but living with all the Denison family.

In Warcop, the Chamley and Preston families lived respectively at Warcop House and Warcop Hall, and the Wyberghs, whose son Frank was a friend of the Breeks' boys and would teach them to shoot and fish, lived at the Old Cottage.

Susan's appearance was practical and uncompromising. I can picture her quite clearly – a small figure, with what I can only describe as a plain, knobbly face, wearing a black cap which was old-fashioned. But she never bothered about her clothes – a pair of stout boots or walking shoes and a long grey skirt with a jacket and blouse. Her eyes twinkled, in the way that the eyes of intensely alive people do. Unlike most of her generation, she was surprisingly untidy (despite the fact that what annoyed her more than anything else were people who would not shut doors!) and judging by her letters, she was always losing things, particularly umbrellas, and forgetting things. Her idea of order, like her visual sense, followed its own laws, guided by expediency and circumstances.

Like all the Denisons, Susan was managing, and coupled with intelligence and curiosity plus a great sense of humour, may have been a little intimidating. But she was tolerant of those older than herself and found the young refreshing. She still had the habit of sitting bolt upright on the floor, which without any support, would seem an agonising position for most of us. I can imagine her writing innumerable letters with papers and books lying all about her.

During the long Westmorland winter, Susan and Liz made a practice of taking the children abroad. As we know from the time of the Dent collapse, Susan had had to manage her financial affairs as economically as she could, and in those days, when the material stability and prosperity of the British Empire was at its height, living and travelling almost anywhere abroad was comparatively cheap. It was the period of a general assumption that every produce throughout the Empire could not but go on getting better – the opulent High Victorian Gothic architecture of Scott, Street and Burgess; the ubiquitous imaginative energy of Dickens or the *Punch* cartoonists; the protectively solid craftsmanship in machine and ornament that had been officially celebrated by the Great Exhibition a quarter of a century before.

The early 1890s in England were peaceful years. Imperialism had run its course, with Kipling as its prophet and Rhodes as its heroic figure. Kruger, the Boer Republican, was yet to appear. The country was preening itself as being one of the richest nations in the world, and yet there were the most dreadful slums and unemployment, so the rich began acquiring a social conscience and taking up social reform. They built flats for the working classes and founded settlements. Money poured into the East End of London. Sargent was the fashionable painter and mauve was the favourite colour of the ladies who, with their hair piled high on their heads, took to cycling, which was then the new rage, and golf, which was the fashionable game. For the majority of people, the Queen had been on the throne for as long as they could remember and life was as secure as it had ever been.

At Edengate, where there was constant coming and going and a good deal of laughter, the fashionable society of the day was left to take care of itself. Life jogged along fairly peacefully. In spite of Susan's energy, good health and wide interests, there is a nostalgia, an echo of the past and, at times, a sadness and loneliness.

In her letters, Susan constantly refers to Ellinor Feilden, wife of the Vicar of the nearby town of Kirkby Stephen, who was a great friend and daughter of Edmund Hornby of Dalton Hall, therefore a cousin of Lady Denison. She and her husband Henry were older than Susan but there was constant coming and going between each other's houses.

A year or two after Susan's return to England, Liz, much to everyone's surprise, became the third wife of the ageing and eccentric Canon Weston, vicar of Crosby Ravensworth, and took Daisy and Birdie Thompson, Jim's niece and nephew, to Crosby Ravensworth with her. Daisy was sent to Cheltenham Ladies College and seems to have taken a violent antipathy towards Canon Weston. Little is known about him except that he had the chancel of the church rebuilt in 1875 and commissioned gargoyles with the sculptured heads of his three wives. Since Liz, his third wife, was still very much alive at the time, even if she was going slightly deaf, it suggests that his was perhaps not the most tactfully accommodating of natures.

Liz, of course, found herself a near neighbour of the Dent family who still lived at Flass. The rift over Dent, Palmer and Co. had fairly soon been healed, thanks principally to the generous attitude of Jim Breeks while he was at Ootacamund, and so Liz was able, without difficulty, to be on good terms with her cousins.

In 1885, the lease on Helbeck had come to an end and Susan moved into the house. Without a doubt, Helbeck appealed to Susan who had shared Jim's romantic leanings. Although she was well aware of the inconvenience after Edengate, she preferred to live apart from what she felt to be the claustrophobic atmosphere of a village where one's every move was instantly observed and speculated upon by close neighbours.

This left Edengate empty and she sold it, using the money, together with a welcome legacy left by Robert Wilkinson, to change the drive up to Helbeck Hall, but none of Jim's more elaborate plans for altering Helbeck were carried out. However, Susan had trees planted in various places on the estate to use as windbreaks and as cover for game (her three sons were, by now, addicted to every sort of shooting and fishing). In the middle of the walled garden, she built a large greenhouse for grapes and peaches. The old entrance yard to the west was grassed over and converted into a tennis court, and along the front of the house, she planted the *Gloire de Dijon* roses which still survive today.

There was a drawing room, dining room, study and billiard room on the ground floor, eight bedrooms above, and the servants slept in the attic. Susan kept a cook, a parlour maid, a housemaid and a scullery maid. This enabled her to live comfortably, but when the house was full, as it often was in the summer, the servants must have been kept very busy.

Outside, there was Jones, the gardener, and Fletcher, the coachman, who lived in the stables with his unruly family. His pride and joy were the four greys which had come from Windsor. In the 1960s, some people still remembered Susan driving these greys.

Inside the house, apart from putting new marble fireplaces in the drawing room and bedrooms above, Susan made hardly any alterations. In particular, the pretty little sitting room at the west end of the house remained as it had been, with its delicate eighteenth century ornamental plaster work, no doubt copied by the local craftsmen from a standard pattern book. This room was Lena's.

In 1886, only a year after moving to Helbeck, Lena, by now a pretty girl of seventeen with a sensitive face and an almost transparently fine skin, died of consumption. She is buried in the churchyard at Brough. The following year, Rosalie, the old family servant who had gone out to Van Dieman's Land with the Denisons forty years earlier, died after a long and painful illness.

The boys' room in the house had its own separate entrance passage from the garden at the back. Superficially perhaps, one of Susan's strangest ideas was to choose a back room, at the north-west corner of the house, for her bedroom. Probably this was so that she could look out on the steep fellside, which she had come to know so well through walks to the Fox Tower with Jim, and which dominates the house so as to give the feeling that one could almost put one's hand out of a back window and feel the mosses and ferns that grow on the jagged half-grassed limestone. Helbeck Wood, into which the fell merges, is a rich, precipitous, natural wood of birch and sycamore, and must in many ways have reminded Susan of the Nilagiris Hills, as would the peacocks which she had introduced into the wood, which bred and naturalised themselves in increasingly large numbers.

In March 1891, Susan was fifty years old. She was constantly on the go and was just as likely to be helping with the hay or cutting nettles as she was to be making one of those interminable afternoon visits. She walked for long distances, rambling in the woods or going to see friends in Warcop. She thought nothing of walking the two miles to church in Brough twice on Sundays, even in the worst weather. She also sketched, read a variety of books, with Kipling being one of her favourites, wrote book reviews, and generally took a great interest in everything that went on, holding strong theological and political views.

By 1895, her sons, Dick and Charles were grown up, though Bill was still at Rugby. None of them really inherited the Denison intellectual interests, being more fond of the country, and fishing and shooting. In fact, shooting was an obsession.

Dick had joined the army in 1893 and in 1895 was 32 years old and a gunner. He was good looking and amiable and was said to have been like his father in looks and ways. He had married Olive Blyth two years earlier in 1893 and they had a daughter, Audrey. Olive was utterly unlike the Breeks or the Denisons. She came from a rich family which Susan described as 'showy' and Susan, who had orthodox views on behaviour, could not have approved. Moreover, Olive had very little in common with Susan or the unfashionable country life which the Breeks's led in Westmorland. She was a very sociable person, mad about horses – she drove a four-in-hand at Olympia. Dick was always a great favourite with his cousin Daisy Thompson, who must have looked upon him more as a brother than a cousin, having been brought up together by their Aunt Liz at Edengate.

Charles, or Carl as he was often called, was 26 years old in 1895 and was vague and amusing. He was fat and had a round, almost Germanic face, very like the Denisons to look at. He had great charm and a sense of humour. He limped because of a club foot and, at this time, was studying medicine in Edinburgh with a friend whom we only hear of as Jack. Charles was the most dedicated shot. He went on shooting and fishing holidays to Iceland, and later spent his holidays big-game shooting in Africa.

Bill, a year younger than Charles, appears to have been the charmer of the family, though delicate and a constant sufferer from headaches and 'liver', which dogged him all his life. He was reading for the bar. At this time, he also painted, and there are still some of his paintings in the attic at Helbeck.

From her letters, it appears that Susan got on well with her sons and her endless worries about their health were not without due cause. She herself had very good health and one can only suppose that all the boys inherited some of their father's weaknesses. All three boys came to Helbeck during the holidays and all three shot extremely well.

Helbeck,
Sunday, (August 1895)

Dearest Lina, [Susan's sister Carolina]

> Bill is a little better but not much and the doctor doesn't know what to make of him, he gets on so slowly. I do hope he will be able to get a little shooting the week after next, but he certainly won't be fit to go out on the twelfth…

There were more grouse at Helbeck in 1895 than there had been in Jim Breeks's time. There were also partridges, pheasants and blackcock. Susan kept a keeper and 50 years ago in Brough it is said that the Breeks's boys thought nothing of going out and shooting a sheep if they felt like it. But this was taken in good heart, for the Breeks boys were 'a good sort' and 'paid for it handsomely.' This no doubt endeared them to the north-countryman who is notoriously careful of his money and wouldn't mind losing a lamb if he was going to make something out of it!

Helbeck in those days was not a dull house! The boys were always coming and going, as well as Susan's numerous brothers and sisters. If she was lonely at times, it was seldom for long as people paid lengthy visits. Every year, her mother, old Lina Denison, came to stay for a long visit and, according to Miss Boswell (a friend of Daisy's) who still remembers these visits, life at Helbeck was not nearly so much fun when old Lady Denison was there. Rather naturally, everything revolved around Lina Denison, who was very stiff and not very easy. Besides, young people are not always tolerant of the old.

Daisy Thompson told me during a conversation I had with her in 1956, "At Helbeck we always walked to church, but when Lady Denison was there, the carriage came around twice."

The harem-scarem way of living at Helbeck was somewhat curtailed and meals had to be at proper times, and for the boys, and the other young ones like Daisy and Peggy, it was always a bore if their visit coincided with the old lady's. Susan made a habit of having her mother to stay in August which couldn't have been more inconvenient with the shooting, but there was no-one left in London in August, and how thankful the Denisons must have been to get out of the city.

Observatory House, which must have been a large, early Victorian house, at East Sheen on the edge of Richmond Park, was sold during the 1880s. Alas, there is nothing left of the original building, the whole area of the house and garden is now a housing estate. One small, modern house, called Observatory House, and a road through semi-detached villas, called Observatory Road, are the only things remaining to remind us of the Denison's home.

In 1895, the Royal Red Book gives Lady Denison and Susan's name as living in London at 196 Cromwell Road. Susan had her own room there, and continued to go several times a year. Today, this house is still just as one would imagine it was then, a large Victorian stucco house with a porch and pillars, like thousands of others that were built all over London during the nineteenth century. The ambivalent attitude that Susan had towards her Aunt Susan and Uncle, the Reverend William Hornby, at St Michael's on Wyre may have been prompted by the realisation that her mother (to whom she was devotedly loyal) and her aunt had always been very close in spirit, even though different in appearance. Lina had lost the ingenuous charm of her youth that came across so well in her early diary. By the mid-1870s, she had become very plain, with her straight hair combed severely back, unlike her sister who, though approximately the same age and by all accounts typically Victorian in social manners, still had a round, attractive face and curls.

The former Caroline Hornby had, at quite an early age, absorbed the ways of colonial society and, after that, never really managed to adapt herself to ordinary well-to-do life in England. The piously respectable atmosphere at St Michael's pleased her,

Susan Breeks with her Windsor Greys.

probably all the more so because it was a well-run household with a footman and numerous servants. However, staying with her daughter at Edengate, not to mention at Helbeck a few years later, was a different matter. Susan sincerely loved her mother and did all she could to make her visits enjoyable.

Like all small villages with several large houses, the occupiers did not always get on. At this time in Warcop, Mr and Mrs Preston were living at Warcop Hall, the Chamleys at Warcop House and the Wyberghs at The Cottage. The Wyberghs had two sons, Hilton and Frank. Frank ran the Burton Estate, he shot and was Master of the Eden Valley Beagles. He and the Breeks boys saw a good deal of each other and it is said that Frank "never did much throughout his life."

Susan was a fervent letter writer and she also kept a copy book. Some idea of what life was like at Helbeck can be gathered from copies of her letters and from her copy book.

Helbeck

Sunday (June 1895)

Dearest Mouse, [Susan's sister Lucy]

What are your plans? The only point that seems at all certain about Dick's is that he can't be here in September so I could very well have you and Kate [Susan's youngest sister] then, or at any time except the last part of August. We are not going to have a large shooting party so I can put up Mamma and Mary [Lady Denison's maid] then but no extra non-shooters.

Did I tell you that Charles has really floated Frank Wybergh. One of his friends, Wotherspoon by name, an Oxford man, has got a sort of agency for a great powder firm and is circulating about these parts advertising it. Charles gave him introductions to the Wyberghs amongst others and between them they have got a sort of agency for Frank, who is to do the same sort of business in Staffordshire

They say it is a very good firm and if a man does well for them they stick to him – so it really is a chance – if he can take it.

Helbeck

June 1895

Dearest Mamma

I think I wrote last on Wed… and what they can mean by 'glaring sun' in London I can't think. My first impression of London was of the dinginess and the extreme pinched look of the houses. One cannot expect anyone to admire London till they know it well enough to feel its size. But as to climate, it is the want of light and colour and the general low tone that strikes me first, I think. It has beauties of its own, as one gradually realises, but is as 'moonlight into sunlight' compared with the tropical and subtropical colourings.

I was rather exasperated by a letter from my new agent, Mr Hesket, coolly suggesting an expenditure of £60 here and £40 there – so I wrote him back an emphatic negative on all but the absolutely indispensable expenditure and took occasion to compare rents now with those of 1880 with the result that I find I have lost over 25 per cent gross rental – a quarter of my land income. No wonder I am pinched – and expenses don't seem to diminish at all – so I shall keep a tight hand on my friend Hesket...

Charles writes that they are moving into their new house, 6 Wemyss Place.

Helbeck
June 1895

Dearest Mamma,

I am sitting out writing this – really so far this is an ideal summer, but it "doesn't do to 'hollo' till you are out of the wood." Bill keeps rather so-so, liver as usual. He is taking violent exercise like Mr Gladstone in cutting trees, greatly to the benefit of my overgrown plantations...

We had a sermon about Joseph's bones this morning... And then we had the usual description of the true Christian who regards the world as a wilderness. "Do I view the world as a vale of tears? Oh, reverend Sir, not I!" one wants to say with Browning's dying man. Of course that sort of twaddle makes Joseph as unreal as the Great Panjandrum – and it is such a very human bit of his story, that longing after the old home of his wandering youth, which would quite make him kin to those people who are keen to be buried with their fathers (even a dry old stick like Uncle Tom [Sir Thomas Wilkinson, brother of Jim's mother] would be buried at Crosby Ravensworth)...

Best love to all – a peacock is chasing the dogs about and disturbing me – I saw two delightful swallows playing with a cat on the way from church – swooping past her nose one after the other while she made ineffectual jumps at them.

Helbeck,
Sunday (June 1895)

Dearest Mouse,

You tell me nothing of George...

Daisy and I drove over to Kirkby on Friday and had tea with Ellinor [Feilden of Kirkby Stephen]. We didn't stay very long but I am afraid too long as I hear she had a headache the next day...

Daisy went back to Penrith for her Sunday duties to my great regret. We tried to arrange for the Dents to come over and pick two new flowers which I have found behind the kitchen garden – a rare orchidaceous thing which Daisy has seen at Whitfield but not in this country...

George was Susan's younger brother. He was living at 196 Cromwell Road with Lady Denison. He was constantly changing jobs, never sticking to anything for long, and he drank. Whitfield Hall in Northumberland was the home of the Rev C E Blackett-Ord, who had married Jim's niece Della Chester.

Helbeck,
Tuesday 25 (June 1895)

Dearest Mamma

I am 'nigh brossen' with the heat – after sauntering about picking flowers and watching haymakers – so I have just turned a basket of roses into the bath to soak and have come to sit under the trees in what breeze there is and try to get cool. Too many flies! I shall have to go in and try to get between window and door somehow. What you are doing in town I can't think, you must be baked alive. I do wish you were here to enjoy this weather – it is scorching and the grass as it stands and my hay would have been better if it had been begun last week, but if the weather holds it will be well got… I am very glad to hear more about George's business. Will you ask him with my love how my '87 port is getting on and when it ought to be moved. I am very glad he is getting plenty of cricket.

Will the girls choose me a shirt with enough decorations in the way of frills or falling collar to be worn without a jacket. These plain ones only do for absolute seclusion and even my grey jacket is too hot now.

Best love to all... I am sending a hamper which is too big for what I want – but boxes are too small – so I must stuff it up somehow – strawberries beginning.

The General Election was to take place in July and Sir Joseph Savory was standing for North Westmorland as a Unionist. Susan wrote to her sister…

> Helbeck,
> Tuesday (June 1895)

Dearest Lina,

Thanks for your letter and thank Mamma for hers. I don't think Ellinor is at all likely to go away for the election… I have promised to lend my carriage to collect voters. We are to have a contest but of course it can only go one way, unless the devil possesses half the Conservatives to stay with their hay.

I have a note from Lady Savory this morning thanking me for the invitation to stay here if convenient and saying they are to sleep at Kirkby but will be glad if they can come to luncheon on their way round.

Heavy showers are deluging the hay rather tiresomely, but I hope every man will do his duty. [Just as the farmer's wives and families helped with the hay, so did Susan.]

I went on Monday to see Mrs Preston who is confined to the house on account of swelling and irritation on her face. However she is much better. Mrs Wybergh was there and tells me that Frank is getting on very well with his new work. He really is to be praised for not taking to drink in the course of eight or nine years of complete idleness in a country village.

> Helbeck
> Saturday (July 1895)

Dearest Mamma,

I have been dividing my time between electioneering and hay since I last wrote… The Savorys turned up to luncheon here just before one and we went down to the old school and found hardly anyone there, most people being at hay.

However in spite of one shower we got all cocked. Dick writes this morning that he will come over to vote on Friday and stay till Monday and I infer that Olive and baby are coming too…

At the General Election when the Unionists got in with a large majority. Susan is obviously delighted with this result and wrote to her sister:

Helbeck,
Sunday (August 1895)

Dearest Lina,

Bill is a good deal better – there is no complication I feared and the faintness is partly accounted for by the medicine being very lowering. It is very tiresome for him just now with the shooting coming on.

…Most mysterious are the ways of the War Office. Dick was to go by train and get the camp ready, then come back to Newcastle and give over the Barracks, back to Morecambe for the practice and then probably back to Newcastle again to ship off the women and children. All their baggage is packed and the wretched creatures are without anything and still no orders have come and they don't know when they will move. No sooner had Dick got to Morecambe than a new order came – the Major must go and give over the Barracks. Dick therefore was to stay at Morecambe. He sent his servant to fetch his luggage and no sooner had the man got to Morecambe than the orders were changed again and he had to go back to Newcastle. And all this commotion is about a regular three years move of a single Battery. What could be done in wartime?

Mamma went off yesterday, the Mouse and I accompanying her…

In August 1895, Kaiser Wilhelm II of Germany was staying with the Earl of Lonsdale at Lowther Castle, and it had been arranged that he should shoot Wemmergill, the grouse moor adjoining that of Helbeck. Lonsdale, the largest landowner in the area and a well-known eccentric, was somewhat disapproved of for his Regency flamboyance and ostentation and nicknamed 'The Yellow Earl' because of his obsessive taste for that colour.

The Breeks boys used to shoot the Helbeck Moor on the same days that Wemmergill was being shot, and if the wind was in the right direction, they had the benefit of Lord Lonsdale's driven birds.

Helbeck, Sunday

Dearest Lina

We are all in great excitement about the German Emperor who is coming to shoot Wemmergill and must of course drive through Brough. Nothing seems to be certain about his plans, not even whether he was to leave the train at Warcop or Kirkby, but our faithful friend Danby came up this morning to see Bill with a paper about the arrangements which he was strictly enjoined to show no-one, by which it appears that the Special will be at Kirkby at 9.28, and another Special an hour earlier with the horses and carriages, so we shall breakfast early and go down to Brough about half past nine to see them pass – I don't know why they keep it such a secret. I shouldn't think there were nihilists or anarchists in these primitive parts – anyway I hope it will be fine – you can't cover butts and it will be rather distressing if he has to shoot in a deluge…

Helbeck,
Monday

Dearest Mamma,

…We have just come back from seeing the Emperor pass. After many contradictory reports we got something solid at last from Bill's friend, Danby the engine driver, who came over to see him yesterday and report that the Emperor's special train was to be at Kirkby at 9:28. Charles declined to wait – but as he drove up past Windmore End to start shooting he might possibly wait by the roadside to see him pass – but I think his desire to get to the back fell before the Baronets will probably overpower him. We breakfasted at half past eight and walked into Brough (Bill and all, and he didn't seem very tired).

Brough has done its little possible in the way of flags – but only seemed able to muster three or four, but everybody was in the street waiting. Mrs Chamley passed us going to the road by the Board school and Lucy and I took our post on the upper cross near the Doctor's house. Olive, Evelyn and Baby, wiser in their generation, climbed higher still where they could see over the hedge and watch the procession down Brough Bank.

We waited about half an hour and then round the corner came first two bicycles from Kirkby, going with all their might. Then two unlucky policemen with drawn swords and poor, fat, brown horses clicking all four feet as they dragged up the hill – how they are to do the remaining seven miles I cannot think. Then three outriders on long latty chestnuts without an ounce of spare flesh – then three carriages each with only a pair of chestnuts – which I thought rather too little, considering the distance. In the first carriage were the Emperor and Lord Lonsdale – he was my side and quite close – but I somehow expected him to be behind, in a procession, and only realised it was him when I saw him lifting his cap.

He has rather the look of Henry Denison – a nice face, I thought – the other carriages were filled with the suite – and heavy enough to be very hard on a pair of horses up three hills. I hardly had a look at them, but Olive says a good many of them were Germans with green felt hats – and that three brakes full of loaders went through before the party with long feathers in their hats.

Another struggling policeman on a still worse horse closed the procession. They were trotting past us, but slowed to a walk before they passed Baby who was occupying a commanding position near the top of the hill, looking with her white perambulator and that large white nurse as if she filled the whole road. She was screaming and kicking with delight at the horses, and the Emperor waved his hand at her and said, "What a jolly baby," while Lord Lonsdale characteristically called to know whose was the chestnut – Dick's new horse which the groom was riding – so Nurse and Groom "wouldn't call the Queen their aunt," as you might imagine.

It came on to rain just after they passed and I sent Baby into Scott's to shelter and called Ida to see her. Ida had been standing in front of her sister-in-law's house and told me she had called out, *Der Kaiser seque Gott* and that he had looked at her and raised his cap, after which she was so excited that she "musste weinen"… I'm afraid the Emperor will have rather a wet day of it… really this is not tempting weather. It is the worst haytime the 'oldest inhabitant' remembers, and showery days like today are really worse than settled rain.

The Emperor comes back between six and seven and I think we shall probably go down and have another look at him.

Helbeck,
Sunday

Dearest Lina

Really, the weather – fine gleams and petting showers reduce everything to a mere sop and destroy all my flowers – it is too provoking. Lucy will have told you of our experiences yesterday morning with the Emperor... We found that Brough had made some efforts at decoration – a line stretched across by the bridge with Ida's *Der Kaiser seque Gott*, white letters on red, and one or two flags and... the Brough band making an effort.

Two of the unhappy policemen who had been with them in the morning appeared, coming back at a foot's pace, and reporting that the party would not be back for about an hour – so we sauntered up the hill and presently met two dismounted policemen perched on a bank on the look-out. They said they had been told that there had been an accident to Lord Lonsdale who had fallen off his horse. This didn't sound likely, and presently a *Penrith Observer* reporter scooting down at best pace to catch the last train said it was one of the Germans which sounded more likely, but we are all convinced that the fall was an explanation and that one of the Germans shot him.

We waited a long time and at last the policemen marched down and said that the procession was in sight – and a cyclist appeared, going at a great pace, and the most dilapidated wreck of a police horse, dead lame and scrambling along in the most painful way with one of the brakes at his heels. Lord Lonsdale was in this, having changed places with someone else, and in one of them the injured man with his head bandaged. The band was doing its best with *God Save the Queen* and the people cheering – thinking that, as before, the Emperor would be in front – there followed a long pause and the band wheezed out – before the scarlet outriders appeared and I was afraid that the real man would get no music whatsoever. However, I trebled them up and they broke into *God Save the Queen* again as he came by. He is rather a nice looking man... I must get the *Penrith Observer* and see what they say about the accident...

Here, as in India, Susan's physical and mental stamina was obviously considerable. As well as becoming an energetic organiser of culture in Brough, she walked a lot – into the woods to sketch or collect flowers, twice to church on Sundays and to Warcop or even Appleby to visit friends. Or she might be scything nettles, lending a hand with the haymaking, campaigning locally at an election, or participating in the village Christmas festivities. Surprisingly, she considered that her own greatest failing was indolence!

Helbeck,
Tuesday (August 1895)

Dearest Mouse,

I did not forget you yesterday and meant to have written to wish you many happy returns but one way and another I was kept on the trot. I had to go down to Brough in the morning and after lunch I drove down to Appleby on a long deferred visit… When I came home I found the boys in the middle of a raid on the pond having nearly emptied it and caught a lot of fish, some for the house and some for the fishpond and I went with them to help extract the victims from some small pools where they were being kept and carry them in cans to the fishpond.

By the end of August, George was back at Helbeck, together with Mouse and Kate.

Helbeck,
September 1895

Dearest Lina,

Many thanks for your letter. Let us hope somebody will enjoy my garden party – I certainly shan't especially as it is raining again today, yesterday having been absolutely cloudless and the unlucky Bill having gone shooting so may not see him again if, as I hope, he gets this appointment. Moreover, unless I can get a fine day or two to mow the lawn and roll it, it will be useless to try and play tennis. Oh dear me it is a trying world. As to your question about the ponds, George says that no doubt if the ponds are full, flood water will come down much quicker.

We spent yesterday chiefly about the garden, except Kate who began a very promising sketch of the castle from near the bridge. It is piping hot and I was worrying round the garden and was close on broke. The boys were toiling all over the high ground and only got five partridges and a brace of blackgame…

Dick writes now that he is likely to be sent off for a course at Shoeburyness instead of coming here in October. Really life is too wearing and I am too cross for anything.

Helbeck,
October 1895

Dearest Lina,

…George and Bill went off yesterday. Poor old George, I am afraid that I must combine to give him a gun and a silver flask and a cigar case. He doesn't seem to have any of these decorations.

Helbeck,
October 1895

Dearest Mamma,

Charles and I started for Penrith in due course for the 2:20 train – he in the meantime secured a splendid hawk, 'Common Buzzard' by the books – but very far from common – one of three that were hovering over our duck. Such beauties that I have charged Ward to let them alone – they are worth a few ducks and rabbits. We have sent the shot one to Rowland Ward to stuff…

I had a talk with Gertrude, [the housemaid] this morning and am relieved to find that she does not mean to marry till March – as she doesn't think winter is a good time to settle into a house. She is inclined to regret not being here next summer to see Alfred…

In the autumn of 1895, Susan was back in London. On her return to Helbeck, she wrote:

November 1895

Dearest Mamma,

I got to Euston in good time and with some difficulty found a place in the single Carlisle carriage, with my face to the engine. As I had been gasping for breath almost in the cab you can imagine I was prepared to go first class rather than sit back. Otherwise it is really a superfluity of extravagance – tell George to go 1st on the NWW. The carriage was carpeted, had a lavatory and was in every respect as good as 1st class. I had rather a stuffy old lady opposite me who was recovering from a cough and wanted the window up, but finding some half-empty carriages at Crewe I changed, not much to the better as to the window…

When I got home Gertrude told me that she had had a telegram from Carl asking when I was to be at home, so I was not surprised though much pleased to get a telegram from him yesterday morning saying he was coming by the half past two train. He looks very well, all the better I suspect for being on the teetotal line – which failing plenty of exercise suits the boys best, I think – very busy at present with Infirmary work…

Helbeck Hall,
3 December, 1895

Dearest Mamma,

I was horrified at getting a telegram yesterday evening from Liz to say she could not come as Henry Chester has had another stroke, and this morning I have another telegram from Daisy to say that there is no hope and he is sinking fast.

Henry Chester, Vicar of Easington in County Durham, died of his stroke three days later, and Susan, among others, attended his funeral. His wife, Mary, was Jim Breeks's sister.

Helbeck

Dearest Mouse,

…I left Easington on Monday by a half past ten train. After much hunting by timetables I found that a route by Stockton would get me to Warcop at half past two… [Warcop was the nearest station to Helbeck].

Poor Mary was very quiet and self-possessed, looking white and thin but keeping pretty well…

Helbeck,
March 1896

Dearest Mamma,

…Still no housemaid or parlour maid. I have at last got a character of the house-maid I had written about but it is to the effect that she is <u>not</u> competent. I don't know whether the supply of good housemaids is running dry or my favourite registry falling off – but I cannot after Gertrude put up with a slovenly housemaid and must wait till I hear of a really good one.

Helbeck,
March 1896

Dearest Mamma,

…When you have finished *The Prisoner of Zenda* please tell Alice to send my book-box back by parcel delivery. I am writing for more books – I hope you like *The Prisoner of Zenda*. I am so glad of the revival of what may be called the romantic novel because that always seems to involve that good old romantic notion of love as something ennobling, and duty as not only supreme but essential to real love. "Loved I not honour more" instead of the low ugly so-called realism which makes love a mere degrading animal passion…

During March 1896, Bill had been in London and ill again. He recovered shortly afterwards and returned to Helbeck. Six months elapsed before Susan continued her copy book.

Helbeck,
August 1896

Dearest Mouse

…Auntie has telegraphed to say that she hopes I am coming, wet or fair. Our guilty consciences have at once jumped to the conclusion that she had something to say to me about Alfred and Daisy and we are on tenter hooks…

In the original letter the words 'Alfred and Daisy' are scratched out by a later hand in ink, but can be made out easily. Alfred was Susan's youngest brother; Daisy was Jim's niece Daisy Thompson.

Helbeck,
September

Dearest Mamma,

…They are all off to the moor this morning and it seems a tolerable day though I am afraid rather too windy… Alfred has accepted, which rather annoys me as he knows Daisy is coming. He has another engagement later on so I don't know how much he is going to see her. I hope he is properly in love and not just inclined to marry – which isn't good enough for Daisy, who will marry with all her heart or not at all. However there are different ways of being in love and Alfred at all events is old enough to know his own mind, but between his love affairs and George's money matters and Bill's uncertain future and all the little frets about the Blyth element in Dick's ménage – and the delays in my own rents – life is beset with anxieties of sorts and I am beginning to think that age develops capacities for worry that used not be in me...

Although she was enchanted by her granddaughter, Audrey, Susan was not a Denison for nothing, and she worried about Audrey because it became clear that she was not hearing anything.

Helbeck,
October

Dearest Mamma,

   Many thanks for your letter. We are a large party now as Auntie, Daisy and Peggy [Peggy Boswell, a friend of Daisy's] all came last night and Alfred this morning at breakfast time. Needless to say one's eyes have been on them all the time, but they both seem quite natural – and Alfred is in no hurry to make advances. I fancy he doesn't want to give himself away before Peggy and the others, for he is this morning sitting with a book in the billiard room. If only I can get Daisy without Peggy when Dick comes back here, we shall have a better chance...

Helbeck,
26th December 1896

Dearest Lina,

   Bitter weather – NE wind and frost and snow flying. It snowed all Christmas Eve but yesterday was fine and we ploughed our way to church – though it was rather cold work sitting with snow-covered boots. The decorations looked very nice... The pillars were done alternately with evergreen wreathing and bands of red like Kirkby pillars, and there was a good deal of red about. I had always been afraid of it because of the red walls, but it looked very well. With the usual slovenliness, only three ringers were there – fancy, in any decent church, the row there would be if any ringer absented himself on Christmas Day...

Helbeck,
27th December 1896

Dearest Mouse

   ...The band came up last night. They have been spending their Christmas holidays in playing all day round the neighbourhood and have raked in quite a large sum – £6 to £8 I believe... I must say people are worth helping who are so willing to help themselves... I suggested that they should go round and have something to drink, but they said they were not "tied to a tune or two" and gave us the tune or two with increasing discordance, after which they went round to the servants' hall and "played gloriously far into the night" dance music, so there was I suppose general jollification. Bill and I performed banjo and piano...

Helbeck,
May 1897

Dearest Mamma,

I have returned to my copying book for the convenience of keeping something answering to a diary. I find that I have got someone else's umbrella, the handle is exactly like mine and I told Sarah [Lady Denison's maid] it was mine, but find that it was in a much better case than mine when I came to look at it. However, as umbrellas are awkward things to send about I think I had better keep it till Bill goes to town.

I was out almost all day yesterday gathering flowers in the wood in the morning for Olive. I will send you some in a day or two. The primroses, when one comes to gather them, are past their best but bluebells and lilies of the valley are beginning. Unluckily the village is getting to know the lily-of-the-valley beds too well and I shall have to say that they are not to be picked next year, I think. It is annoying to find them completely rifled when one comes to them. As I was sitting on a bank picking primroses I heard quite a thumping noise underneath me, and after a little listening thought it was the stamp of a buck rabbit in his burrow – but it might really have been the Queen in *Alice,* it quite suggested fairyland underground.

Bill well and cycling vigorously.

Helbeck,
May

Dearest Mamma,

I think that I have only written a scrap or two since Sunday – or was it Monday? It must have been that night when a sudden tempest of worrying snarls arose from the smoking room and I, rushing in with a lamp, found that Jossy and Spot had got together unknown and were scrimmaging over books and cartridge boxes. I seized Spot by the neck and vainly screamed to the maids to collar Jossy – even the great Gertrude can't realise that if she will only get a dog by its throat he can't bite her. However, they were not in such deadly earnest as they sometimes are and Jossy allowed himself to be hustled out, while I held Spot who has taken the adventure so ill that he has been in Brough ever since till tonight.

Helbeck,

Dearest ??

Lucy is writing to Lina and will have told her of our conversation with Liz yesterday and our fears that Daisy would never marry while she lived because she always asks herself whether she would marry so and so to leave Liz – I mean whether she can really be happier with the lover who present himself, and thitherto this has been fatal.

Of course this may not be so with Alfred and I think he might have a chance if he lets her know what he wants, and is willing to wait. He will not get her now but he might eventually. Liz would probably be on his side as she is anxious that he should marry. The worst of it is that every year makes Liz more dependent on

Daisy, as she gets older and more rheumatic, and I am sometimes afraid that it may not come off in her lifetime.

Alfred and Daisy never did marry. It is evident that Daisy Thompson ultimately identified herself with the older generation. She remained devoted to Liz and though nearly a quarter of a century younger than Susan, shared her catholic interests and was a very frequent visitor to Helbeck. Together they hunted for rare wild flowers in the wood, organised choral singing and neither of them wavered at getting up at four o'clock in the morning to go and watch the sunrise from the top of Mount Ida, a high hill behind the house. Daisy and her friend, Peggy Boswell, like many young ladies in that period, vigorously took to cycling and thought nothing of riding twenty miles at a time, cycling from Penrith to Helbeck.

Helbeck,
January 1897

Dearest Mouse,
    …If <u>only</u> there is no war… Poor Jameson – one's heart aches for him. I wish he had been killed – to have ruined oneself is bad enough but to have brought half a continent into confusion – ruined his friend Rhodes (not but what I believe Rhodes was in it) and blown up the Company and all, far worse than nothing, it is terrible to live after that. I think the Uitlanders come very badly out of it and don't need any help. I shall waste no tears on their screams.

Dr Jameson's party, coming to the aid of the Uitlanders, was defeated by the Boers near Krugersdorp and surrendered on 2nd January. Jameson however was released a week later.

Helbeck,
January 1897

Dearest Mamma,
    I am very glad you are better but it is a pity you cannot go down to the dance, which you would have enjoyed. You aught to have a select party in your room of the chaperones you know best… I am relieved by this morning's news – anyhow Jameson is safe and as for the Uitlanders, they have made their own foolish bed and must lie in it.
    I haven't heard from Dick since he got back, he was very sorry to leave me, as he said, with the Boers! I enjoyed having him immensely in spite of our public miseries – he gets more and more like Jim in many ways…

In the summer of 1897, Susan visited London to witness Queen Victoria's Jubilee celebrations. She wrote to Bill with lengthy descriptions of the event:

196 Cromwell Road,
21 June 1897

Dearest Bill,

I am going to write my account of the Jubilee to you by means of this copying book as I think these "Leaves from a private diary" may be interesting to my grandchildren one day. Dick came here yesterday with fever on him after Ascot. He says that from where they were on Cup day they couldn't see when Persimmon (the Prince of Wales's horse) came to the front, but they heard at once by the <u>roar</u> that swept along with the horse, and when he came in the whole crowd surged over and past the police and went and yelled in front of the Prince's box. He had a violent row with a whole carriage full of Blyths who were ill-advised enough to say the Queen was stingy – and scolded them till they fled…

I don't generally like London in summer – but I must say that London *en fête* is charming. The decorations are patchy and scrappy, I admit – one house covered with flags, the next with nothing – but there is a general air of excitement and good nature all over, brakes full of country people and sightseers in all directions, people running about with flags and wires for lamps – Jubilee ribbons on everyone and everything, Royal carriages in all directions and sentries in all sorts of unexpected corners keeping watch over hotels containing foreign royalties and sorts. We asked a soldier today at a corner in Grosvenor Place who he was guarding and he said he didn't know!

Grandma and I went for a drive along the route on Saturday and came in for a bit of excitement. I saw the wreaths of smoke and tongues of flame shooting out from a house and began to think however that a fire engine would be along, but when we came up it was only the decorations round the window which were burning… So we went to Uncle Henry's church, [Susan's brother, Rev Henry Denison] and never was I so nearly striking my heart's beloved Mahatma. Would you believe that he didn't in his sermon say one syllable about the Jubilee but was paddling on about Corpus Christi all the time – which he can do any year and nobody wanted to hear about. Certainly we sang *God Save the Queen* with a will at the end, but on the whole I was very cross – only it isn't possible to be angry with Uncle Henry for very long…

This morning, poor little Alfred Austin had published his Jubilee ode, which for a laureate thing isn't bad, "Rules over half the land and all the sea" isn't a bad idea.

Directly after breakfast we all started off to see Her Majesty come in, and go standing room half way down Constitution Hill. We had to stand for an hour and a half – but in a most good natured, amusing crowd – the women took off their hats to let people see, and there was a charming old man near me who had come a long way, he said – he did just want to see the Queen; he kept giving up his place to women, so I was afraid he wouldn't see, but when she passed I turned round and saw him grinning with delight and saying that he had seen her very well. We were kept amused by all sorts of Royal carriages flashing by.

The strain on the royal stables is such that Dick says that one of the Woolwich Batteries has been unhorsed and all the drivers taken on as postillions, much to their delight. Moreover, besides the regular scarlet people a lot of private hansoms are being used for the smaller fry, the drivers having a royal badge on plain black livery and a crown on the cab.

At last we heard hurrahs creeping on and the escort came by at a trot and then the open carriage and four – with Her Majesty on our side so that we got an excellent sight of her. Did you hear that the survivors of the Balaclava Charge have been collected and given a window to themselves? They expressed themselves very anxious that the Queen should look their way when she comes by tomorrow – and she has taken note of their place and promised to look at them. We all prepared to cry *God Save the Queen* as she passed – but our efforts were quite drowned in the screams of an enthusiastic woman next to me. George's friend, Kangaroo Bill, is here – a pleasant looking man. I am glad to know that his name is Nash as one can't address him as Kangaroo Bill

The *Yorkshire Post* has it that the Helbeck fells are to have a line of fire from Mt Ida to Malplaquet. Did you ever hear of Malplaquet?

Best Love; I will write again after the show.

It is surprising that Susan did not know of Malplaquet, the name of a part of the fellside at the back of Helbeck. It is not marked on any map; but then neither is Mount Ida, and both names have survived in local parlance to this day and are always used by the local hunt.

196 Cromwell Road,
22 June 1897

Dearest Bill,

...Well, it is all over and a splendid sight, but we came very near losing it owing to Sir E Bradford's advice that we should follow the route of the procession. We were all quite punctual and left the house at a quarter past seven – Grandma, Uncle Henry and Aunt Lina in the carriage and the rest of us in an omnibus. At half past seven we were at the Alexandria Hotel or thereabouts – and at half past eight we were only at Hyde Park Corner.

We were told that if we got into the line of route we should be passed on if we got far enough – but we were only at the beginning and were inexorably swept into the park. Here the block was almost worst – carriages going all ways – people were getting out in despair and walking. Deep despair fell on us all – the block at Hyde Park Corner had been caused by all the cavalry who had camped there filing out. Now that we had got into the park, behold, all the Infantry were turning out by Stanhope Gate and again we had to sit and swear.

At last there was a move and our man with great judgement fled along to a higher gate and cut across empty side streets through Leicester Square; we got out at the top of Bow Street and went down on foot. With our cards we were passed across, although the streets were already lined with soldiers. The Strand, as one glanced up and down in crossing, was a beautiful picture – the open gravelled space in the middle with the lines of scarlet on each side – the many coloured flags on the houses and the green wreaths streaming from mast to mast right along the street.

When we got in we had another moment of anguish because Grandma hadn't turned up, but just as we were wailing and tearing our hair, we saw the line of soldiers butted apart by Uncle Henry with Grandma on his arm and Aunt Lina following, so we were at peace and could enjoy the sight. I shall be curious to see by the papers if anyone lost their seats altogether. There were crowds behind us. If only they had arranged different lines of approach for different parts of the route, everybody could have got along, for there was no crush whatever in the side streets; it seems to have been the one mistake of the arrangements.

Once settled, the time seemed quite short. First, carriages with the invited guests for St Paul's came rolling past, ambassadors and dignitaries in Windsor uniform and feathered hats and all sorts of finery – then came sailors marching to take their place somewhere near St Paul's, and volunteers also. Then after a bit came the Band and an escort of Life Guards – ADCs and Generals of sorts – so confusing that we thought we had missed Bobs [Field Marshal Lord Roberts] – but not a clear space followed, and there was the little old man on a white horse, alone, getting a tremendous reception; I was so pleased.

Then followed the Colonials, and even I was satisfied with the applause they got. First a lot of Canadian mounted troops – some in red and some in blue – then a royal carriage with splendidly harnessed horses and Laurier who got, as I expected, the honours of the Procession – a sharp faced, keen looking man in Windsor uniform, bowing as he went. Then came the Cornstalks and really they did look fine. There is something so workmanlike about that brown khaki and the sombrero hats on these splendid men too.

The New South Wales men had feathers on one side, the Victorians a sort of crimson ball on the top which is not so pretty – but it is most effective altogether. The Canadian uniform, as is natural, is more like ours, with helmets or busbies – but these lean brown men with their slouch hats seem to belong to quite another world – a wild, rougher life, somehow they suggest long rides on burnt plains and headlong hunts after bushrangers and miles of unexplored country. NSW and Victoria each had a carriage to himself, the smaller colonies double up – all got a splendid reception – a great enthusiasm greeted the Rhodesian horse headed by Capt Gifford with his empty sleeve. They say that the East End warmed up to him more than anything.

After this, one got a little confused. Sikhs and Chinese – browns and blacks of all sorts followed one another in perplexing numbers – lots of tall blacks, and we could not distinguish the dear Niger Hausas to whom we wanted to give a special greeting. Hong Kong was curious to look at – gigantic Sikhs marching alongside those pygmy Chinamen with their parchment skin and their perfectly inexpressive faces...

We thought there would be a pause before the royal procession, but before you could say knife, the "biggest officer in the British Army" was upon us with his half dozen guards, then Cavalry bands, Cavalry squadrons, three by three with batteries of HM Artillery between them (sailors first, by the way), and then all those beautiful creatures – every buckle shining like silver, bands with silver kettle drums – the Waterloo Brigade together. First, Dragoons, Scots Greys and Iniskillins – a Dragoon again, Hussars, Lancers, including the Balaclava 17th who got an extra reception...

…Then another string of royal carriages – no, then the Colonial Escort – then the carriages with… Mostly in uniforms; but actual Royalties began, first a charming lot of the Battenburg, Connaught and Coburg children, all bowing as prettily as possible, then Hesses and Denmarks and Lecks and Coburgs all in their order till the last carriage held the actual children of the Queen – and the last of all with four splendid blacks and two walking footmen held the Empress Frederick.

Then came the escort of Princes and again we were quite maddened by the impossibility of distinguishing them. One little Oriental, perhaps the Siamese Prince, was riding a lovely Arab pony, a perfect little creature, and there were again all sorts of strange and splendid uniforms. Then the Indian Escort – magnificent. But, all this time one was quite shaken with the roar that came surging along from behind, accompanying the Queen. All the combined cheers that had been given to all the others in one didn't touch this – from the head of the first cream till the carriage was out of sight it was one roar, and then one heard it rolling on and on. Even the Prince of Wales riding behind passed quite unnoticed.

The Princess of Wales and the Princess Christian were sitting on the opposite seat – and the creams were absolutely covered with trappings. Altogether it was a wonderful sight and a proud one. The procession being so much longer there was nothing like the squash there was in places last time – nobody was squeezed – and as always on these occasions everyone was good-humoured. Some people opposite us who had some spare places at the Gaiety picked up children out of the crowd and gave them seats. Mrs Warre, who was one of the party, told me that she had been watching some do of this kind beside an American woman, who after watching the good-humoured way in which the police managed the crowd, said, "Well, I never saw anything like this; in our country the police would have had their clubs out long ago, and had to use them too," she added…

196 Cromwell Road,
25 June 1897

Dearest Bill,

I suppose you and Carl are rambling somewhere, as I have no answer to my telegram…

I hope you had the thunderstorm which made London bearable, the heat till now has been very trying – if only society would let one go about in a nightgown what a boon it would be. Jubilee and again Jubilee – for once we reputedly solid people have fairly lost our heads and are still holiday-making. As for the Stock Exchange and the City, generally nothing is doing at all. On Saturday they were taking ladies to see the decorations – on Monday they met only to send addresses and sing *God Save the Queen* – on Tuesday of course they were jubilating – on Wednesday they were courteously, the Germans full of fussy protestations that they are, or will be, quite as great if people only knew it. As for ourselves, the intoxication of pride and delight seems to have taken the place of ordinary drink and the police and magistrates have nothing to do. Everybody grins and cheers, everybody is good-humoured and happy – there is a sort of indescribable thrill that is going through everybody, as if we too had suddenly waked up to find ourselves supreme – unique in our Empire, our Queen…

Got Carl's telegram so shall go home on Monday.

~ ~

Two years later, in 1899, Lady Denison died at Helbeck during her annual summer visit. She had almost completely lost touch with life at Knowsley, where she had regularly stayed as a child. Her sister, Susan Hornby, did remain in touch, partly because her son was agent there and partly because the Hornbys lived in the same country and mixed with the same society, as well as being relations. But Lady Denison had been abroad and did not, on her return, make any attempt to restore connections with the Derby family. Susan Breeks, therefore, probably knew nothing about her grandmother Maria Burgoyne's childhood. How she would have judged them from the standpoint of 1899 is open to speculation, but she would have been genuinely and unashamedly interested.

I think the Denisons must have been a very alarming family. They are remembered as being very managing and, like Susan, interested in music and the arts. The eldest Lucy, or Mouse, who was only a little over four feet tall and was really a midget. In 1899, she was 54 years old and she, of all the sisters, would be the one who could clearly remember their childhood in India. She was a great character and most amusing, and she wore a wig with a big bun on the top. She was delicate and, like her sisters, did beautiful needlework and sketched and drew very well.

Lina, the next daughter, was 49. She was the least managing of them all, but the most attractive, the least intellectual and the easiest to get on with. I have seen a photograph of Lina as a very good looking old lady, in the garden at Ossington, taken many years later. She was the best of them all at needlework and invented a stitch which was used by them all in the making of innumerable altar frontals, stoles and other church work. 'Denison' work is, I am told, still recognised by some to this day. There is a piece of work in the church at Brough, which was said to have been used on Lina's coffin. This may well have been 'Denison' work.

Kate was by far the youngest of Lady Denison's children, and at 39 was only a little older than Dick and Daisy. She too was delicate and had a cast in her eye, but she was a great character and, like her elder sister Mouse, spent a great deal of time drawing. All the sisters were musical and Kate had a very good voice, and singing still being the fashion must have been a help, especially to Kate whose looks were described as "all teeth and nose."

Henry was the greatest charmer of the family. As a little boy, at the age of eight, he played the organ beautifully and had a piano specially made for him so that his feet could reach the pedals! He was very clever and wrote theological books. He painted the interiors of churches in his spare time, but it was as an organist he excelled. In 1895 he was Curate to his uncle Archdeacon Denison at East Brent in Somerset and every

Sunday the church would be packed as people liked to come from afar to hear Henry play the organ. Everyone who can remember him speaks of him with great affection and he was described as 'a dear'.

James, another brother, had died in 1887 when he was Provost of Cuddesdon Theological College.

George seems to have been living at Cromwell Road with all his sisters. He was the ne'er do well – the one who was so totally different to the others. He has been described to me as looking like Edward VII when he was young. He was already taking to drink. He could never hold down a job and, having spent several years in South America as an engineer, he seems to have returned to England and never done anything else, other than be rather a problem to them all. However, he quite often came to Helbeck where his engineering knowledge was put to good use in damming ponds and laying drains. Although details are never mentioned, his sister's letters speak of him with genuine affection as opposed to merely pity, but the pathos remains.

Alfred, the youngest brother, was I think Susan's favourite and when he was in England, made his home at Helbeck. In 1895, he was 39 years old and was a tea planter in Ceylon (now Sri Lanka). It is nice to know there is, to this day, a tea estate in Ceylon which is called Helbeck as he, like so many planters, called their estates after their homes in England. Alfred was the easiest of them all and Susan herself said he had more of the social graces than most of them and a fund of small talk. Certainly people in Westmorland were very anxious to see him when he came home.

The only one to marry, besides Susan, was Willy. He had married Lady Elinor Amhurst and inherited Ossington from his uncle, John Denison, the first Lord of Ossington, but whose widow still lived there. Susan hardly mentions Willy in her letters.

In 1899 Liz was now 68 and becoming deaf. Canon Weston had died fairly soon after he married her, and she and Daisy now lived at a small house called Ashbank in Penrith, which Liz had taken while looking for something else. The 'something else' never materialised and she and Daisy lived on at Ashbank, a small, square, plain house near the railway station with a room on either side of the front door. I can remember some rather pokey rooms at the back and distinctly remember two huge bearskins which hung on the stairs.

Daisy, though years younger than Susan, was a great friend and frequently stayed at Helbeck. She was 35 and was interested in all the things Susan liked and together they went botanising and singing and organising choirs. Both were well informed and read a great deal.

By then Susan's grandparents (Phipps and Maria Hornby) were both dead and the old Wilkinson Uncles had also all died. Winwick, Little Green and those large London houses in Cumberland Place had merged into the past. A new generation lives there now.

The final letter of Susan's surviving copy books was written to her sister Lina in January 1901.

Helbeck,
17 January 1901

Dearest Lina,

I presume you are at home again though you never said how long you were going to be at Ossington. I went to Kirkby last night to hear Miss Wakefield lecture on North Country music – a very good and interesting lecture. I didn't know before that *Barbara Allen* was a border song and that *Scarlet Town* was meant to be Carlisle. She sang it to a Border tune but not as good as our old one, but still a very good tune. Some of the tunes were old 'Rants' or dances – she gave us the original rant from which *John Peel* is derived and remarked more than once that the Scotch have laid claim to several tunes which don't belong to them "keeping the sawbath and everything else they can lay hold of" amongst others to the *Keel Row* which is a Tyneside song. *Moppen I May* is a charming dialect song and she wound up with *Sally Grey.*

Ellinor has had an arrack for gout, which she says has done her good; she has been delighting in the frost and east winds which unluckily has changed and we have gone back to soft cloudy weather. What do you think about *Henry V*? Is it worth going to see? If so we might do it while I am with you…

I went to see my Australian acquaintance in Musgrave and rather sympathise. She is not a lady, but she married in Australia where I infer her husband had a tolerable position and comes home to find all his relations are farmers. I don't quite know what to do with her or for her now I have made her acquaintance either.

Best love to all.

Five days later, the Queen, by now a very old lady but still signing official documents, died at Osborne in the arms of her grandson Kaiser Wilhelm of Germany.

Was this the end of an era for Susan Breeks? The fact remains that despite her interest in people, she was solitary by instinct, and that despite the changing climate of English fashionable society, the peaceful, mildly irregular life of Helbeck was to continue for some time to come, much as it had been for the previous sixteen years. Susan was now sixty and leaving home less and less. For the rest of her life she walked, sketched, worked on the estate and travelled abroad a little…

Susan died in 1923 at Ashbank.

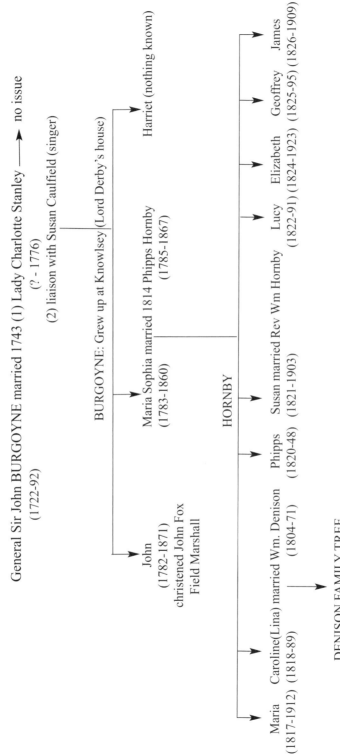

BURGOYNE FAMILY TREE

General Sir John BURGOYNE married 1743 (1) Lady Charlotte Stanley ⟶ no issue
(1722-92)   (? - 1776)
                                      (2) liaison with Susan Caulfield (singer)

BURGOYNE: Grew up at Knowlsey (Lord Derby's house)

Harriet (nothing known)

John   Maria Sophia married 1814 Phipps Hornby
(1782-1871)   (1783-1860)   (1785-1867)
christened John Fox
Field Marshall

HORNBY

Maria   Caroline(Lina) married Wm. Denison   Phipps   Susan married Rev Wm Hornby   Lucy   Elizabeth   Geoffrey   James
(1817-1912)   (1818-89)   (1804-71)   (1820-48) (1821-1903)   (1822-91) (1824-1923) (1825-95)   (1826-1909)

                                      DENISON FAMILY TREE

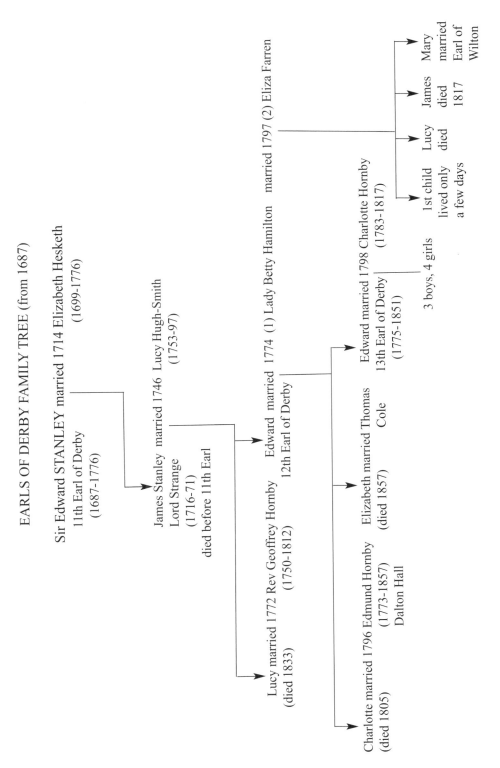

EARLS OF DERBY FAMILY TREE (from 1687)

Sir Edward STANLEY married 1714 Elizabeth Hesketh
11th Earl of Derby   (1699-1776)
(1687-1776)

James Stanley married 1746 Lucy Hugh-Smith
Lord Strange   (1753-97)
(1716-71)
died before 11th Earl

Lucy married 1772 Rev Geoffrey Hornby   Edward married 1774 (1) Lady Betty Hamilton   married 1797 (2) Eliza Farren
(died 1833)   (1750-1812)   12th Earl of Derby

Charlotte married 1796 Edmund Hornby   Elizabeth married Thomas   Edward married 1798 Charlotte Hornby
(died 1805)   (1773-1857)   Cole   13th Earl of Derby   (1783-1817)
                            Dalton Hall   (died 1857)   (1775-1851)

3 boys, 4 girls

1st child   Lucy   James   Mary
lived only   died   died   married
a few days   1817   Earl of
                                        Wilton

HORNBY FAMILY TREE (from 1750)

Rev. Geoffrey HORNBY (Rector of Winwick) married 1772 Lucy Stanley (sister of Edward, 12th Earl of Derby)
(1750-1812)   (? - 1833)

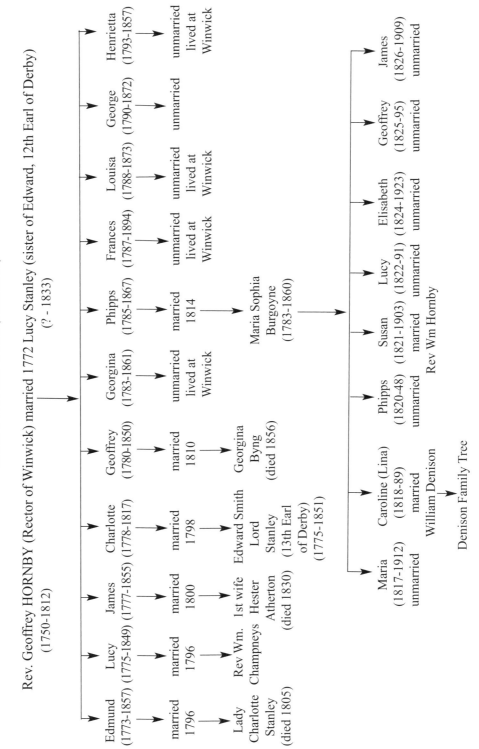

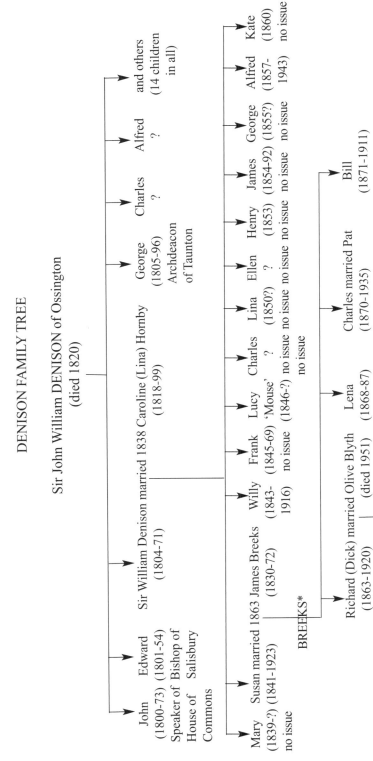

DENISON FAMILY TREE

Sir John William DENISON of Ossington
(died 1820)

John
(1800-73)
Speaker of
House of
Commons

Edward
(1801-54)
Bishop of
Salisbury

Sir William Denison married 1838 Caroline (Lina) Hornby
(1804-71)   (1818-99)

George
(1805-96)
Archdeacon
of Taunton

Charles
?

Alfred
?

and others
(14 children
in all)

Mary
(1839-?)
no issue

Susan married 1863 James Breeks
(1841-1923)   (1830-72)

BREEKS*

Willy
(1843-
1916)

Frank
(1845-69)
no issue

Lucy
'Mouse'
(1846-?)

Charles
?
no issue

Lina
(1850?)
no issue

Ellen
?
no issue

Henry
(1853)
no issue

James
(1854-92)
no issue

George
(1855?)
no issue

Alfred
(1857-
1943)

Kate
(1860)
no issue

Richard (Dick) married Olive Blyth
(1863-1920)   (died 1951)

Audrey
(died 1951)

Lena
(1868-87)
no issue

Charles married Pat
(1870-1935)
no issue

Bill
(1871-1911)
no issue

* see Breeks Family Tree

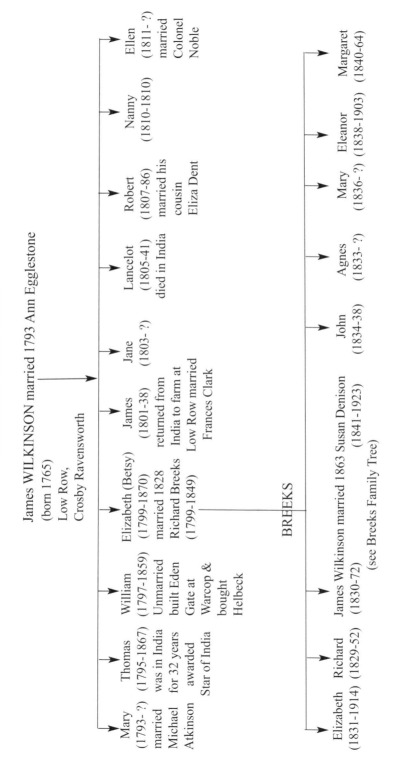

WILKINSON FAMILY TREE

James WILKINSON married 1793 Ann Egglestone
(born 1765)
Low Row,
Crosby Ravensworth

Mary
(1793- ?)
married
Michael
Atkinson

Thomas
(1795-1867)
was in India
for 32 years
awarded
Star of India

William
(1797-1859)
Unmarried
built Eden
Gate at
Warcop &
bought
Helbeck

Elizabeth (Betsy)
(1799-1870)
married 1828
Richard Breeks
(1799-1849)

James
(1801-38)
returned from
India to farm at
Low Row married
Frances Clark

Jane
(1803- ?)

Lancelot
(1805-41)
died in India

Robert
(1807-86)
married his
cousin
Eliza Dent

Nanny
(1810-1810)

Ellen
(1811- ?)
married
Colonel
Noble

BREEKS

(see Breeks Family Tree)

James Wilkinson married 1863 Susan Denison
(1830-72)   (1841-1923)

Elizabeth   Richard
(1831-1914) (1829-52)

John
(1834-38)

Agnes
(1833- ?)

Mary
(1836- ?)

Eleanor
(1838-1903)

Margaret
(1840-64)

BREEKS FAMILY TREE

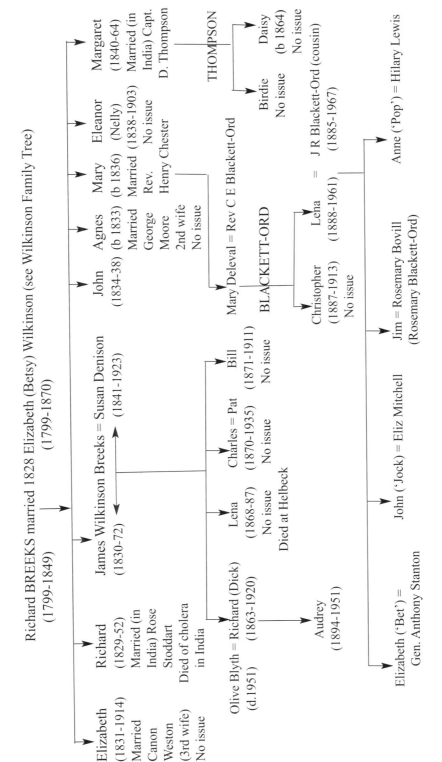

Bibliography

ENGLAND:

Beaumont, William, *Winwick: Its History and Antiquities,* 1875.

Beauties of England and Wales, Lancashire, Surry and Westmorland, 1815.

Bovill, E. W., *English Country Life,* 1962.

Briggs, A. S. A., *The Age of Improvement.*

Bulmer's Directory of Westmorland, 1885 and 1887.

Cobbett, William, *Rural Rides in England,* 1821.

Ferguson, Richard, *County of Westmorland*, 1894.

Garnett, F. W., *Westmorland Agriculture, 1800-1900.*

Guide Book to Knowsley Hall, 1955.

Hodgson, Rev. J., *County of Westmorland*, 1813.

Hoskins, W. G., *The Making of the English Landscape.*

Howett, William, *Rural Life in England*, Vols. I and II, 1838.

Johnson, W., *England As It Is*, 1851.

Memorials of Haileybury College, 1894.

Nicolson, Joseph, and Burn, Richard, *History and Antiquities of Westmorland and Cumberland*, 1777.

Parkinson, Richard, *Guide and History of Kirkby Stephen.*

Stephens, Henry, *The Book of the Farm*, Second edition, 1852.

Sullivan, J., *Cumberland and Westmorland – Ancient and Modern*, 1857.

Thompson, F. M. L., *English Landed Gentry in the 19th Century.*

Wilson, W., *Coaching Past and Present.*

Young, G. M., *Victorian England.*

The London Library.

Private family papers.

INDIA AND THE EAST

Anderson, A., *A Cruise on an Opium Clipper.*

Atkinson, J., *Curry and Rice,* 1851.

Blaikie, R., *Observations of the Neilgherries,* 1834.

Breeks, J. W., *The Primitive Tribes of the Nilagiris,* 1873.

Burton, Richard, *Goa and the Blue Mountains,* 1851.

Carey, W. H., *The Good Old Days of the John Company,* 1906.

Campbell, G., *Modern India,* 1852.

Cleghorn, Hugh, *Forest and Gardens of South India,* 1861.

Dodwell, H., *The Nabobs of Madras,* 1926.

East India Register and Army List, 1857.

Eden, Emily, *Up the Country, 1837-1840.*

Edwards, Michael, *Bound to Exile,* 1969.
Edwards, Michael, *British India, 1772-1947,* 1947.
Fergusson, *Directory of Ceylon*, 1906.
Foster, Sir Wm., *John Company.*
Foster, Sir Wm., *The East India House.*
Hickey, William, *Memoirs.*
Holmes, Rice, *Cambridge History of India,* 1922.
Jones, Clement, *A Chief Officer in China.*
Lubbeck, Basil, *The Opium Clipper.*
Maitland, T. C., *Letters from Madras – By a Lady.*
Panter Downes, Molly, *Ooty Preserved,* 1967.
Postans, Mrs., *Western India,* 1838.
Price, Sir Frederick, *Ootacamund,* 1908.
Spear, G. P., *The Nabobs,* 1832.
Roberts, Field Marshall Lord of Kandhar, *Forty-One Years in India,* 1897.
Vansittart, Jane, *From Minnie with Love: Letters of Maria Wood, 1849-1861.*
Williamson, T., *The East Indian Vade Mecum: A Compendium of Information for Officers of the Company Going Out to India.*
Woodruff, Philip, *The Guardians.*
Woodruff, Philip, *The Men Who Ruled India*
Woodruff, Philip, *The Founders of South India,* 1861.

AUSTRALIA AND TASMANIA
Adams, David, *The Letters of Rachel Henning, 1853-82*
Capper, J., *Emigrants Guide to Australia,* 1852.
Casey, E. M. S., *Australian Story, 1837-1907.*
Early Buildings of Southern Tasmania, pub. Melbourne.
Mossman, S. and Bannister T., *Australia Visited and Revisited*, 1853.
Nugent, Lady Maria, *Journal 1801-15*, 2 Volumes, 1839.
Scholes, Arthur, *The Sixth Continent,* 1958.
Silver's *Handbook for Australia*, 1874.
Tasmania (Van Dieman's Land), *Country Life* magazine, October-November 1974.
Whiteside, Capt. A. *Journal of a Voyage in the Barque Parkville from Plymouth to   Australia*, 1843.

THEATRE
The Garrick Stage and Theatres
Intimate Society Letters
The Stanleys of Knowsley
The Testimony of Truth to Exalted Merit: A biographical sketch of the Honourable Countess of Derby in refutation of a false and scandalous libel, 1797.
Bloxham, Suzanne, *Walpole's Queen of Comedy, Elizabeth Farren,* 1988.
Burny, Charles, *Theatrical Register (1777-97).*
Creevey, Thomas, Papers: Ed. Sir John Gore, 1948.
Creevey, Thomas, Papers: Ed. Sir Herbert Maxwell, 1903.
Cox, Millard, *The Life and Times of the 12th Earl of Derby.*

Denison, Sir William, *Varieties of Vice Regal Life,* 1870.
Farrington, Joseph, *Diaries.*
Fyvie, John, *Comedy Queen of the Georgian Era,* 1906.
Grenville, Charles, Ed. Henry Reeve, Vol. VIII, 1820-1900.
Holtzman, J. M., *The Nabobs in England,* 1926.
Hudleston, F. J., *Gentleman Johnny Burgoyne.*
Kelly, Linda, *The Kemble Era,* 1980.
Mellon, M. R. S., *Marriage from the Stage,* 1847.
Noakes, Vivien, *Edward Lear,* 1985.
Nugent, Lady Maria, *Journal 1801-15,* 1839.
Pain, Laurian, *'Gentleman Johnny' – Life of General John Burgoyne.*
Pocock, Tom, *Remember Nelson.*
Pollard, W., *History of the Stanleys of Knowsley,* 1863.
Smiles, Samuel, *George Moore.*
Tomalin, Claire, *Mrs. Jordan's Profession,* 1994.
Walpole, Horace, Letters Ed. Peter Cunningham, 1857.

LETTERS AND PAPERS
Breeks, James Wilkinson, Letters
Breeks, Susan, Letters
Breeks, Elisabeth, Letters
Burgoyne, General Sir John, Letters
Creevey, Thomas, Letters
Denison, Lady (Lina), *Reflections on Early Life.*
Farren, Miss Eliza, Letters
Hornby, Lady (Lina), *Grandma's Legacy: Extracts of Letters to her daughter Caroline Denison.*
Hornby, Rev. George, Notebook.
Wilkinson, William, Account Books, 1852.
12th Earl of Derby, Letters and Diaries.

CUMBRIAN HISTORY
Bulmer's *Directory of Westmorland.*
Census Returns.
Dictionary of National Biography.
Gentleman's Magazine, 1774 and 1792.
Illustrated London News (various).
Kelly's *Directory of Westmorland and Cumberland* (various dates).
Post Office Directories, 1830 onwards (various).
Royal Red Book, 1895.
The Cumberland and Westmorland Herald (various).
The Times newspapers (various).
The Transactions, Cumberland and Westmorland Antiquarian and Archaeological Society (various).

Index